# SUCCESSFUL
*projects*

ISBN-13: 978-1-7324139-1-7
ISBN-10: 1-7324139-1-6

Published by:
Successful Projects Press
PO Box 1341
Dripping Springs, TX 78620
email: info@successfulprojects.com
www.successfulprojects.com


@2018 Successful Projects, LLC. All rights reserved.


Successful Projects, LLC content is copyright protected by U.S. intellectual property law that is recognized by most countries. To republish or reproduce Successful Projects' content, you must obtain our permission.

For pricing information or other inquiries, please contact Successful Projects Press.
Printed in the United States of America. No part of this work may be reproduced or transmitted in any form or by any means, electronic, manual, photocopying, recording, or by any information storage and retrieval system, without the prior written permission of the publisher.

PMP and PMBOK are registered marks of the Project Management Institute, Inc.

## About the Author and Successful Projects

Renee Adair is the Owner/President of Successful Projects, LLC.

She has over 25 years of project management experience. She has a bachelor's degree in Business Administration and her Project Management Professional (PMP®) certification through the Project Management Institute (PMI®). She is active with the PMI local Austin Texas chapter at the board level, as well as with International Project Management Day.

She is the Director of the Certificate in Project Management program that is offered through six Universities in Wisconsin: UW-Eau Claire, UW-La Crosse, UW-Green Bay, UW-Stout, UW-Stevens Point, UW-Superior, as well as through Texas A&M University, Loraine County Community College and the Northwest New Jersey Small Business Development Center.

Renee's project management background also includes extensive experience in project management contracting, and project management coaching. All workbook readers should feel free to contact Renee regarding any questions, or for project advice, tools and templates, and additional resources.

Contact Information:
Renee Adair, PMP
Owner
Successful Projects, LLC
P.O. Box 1341
Dripping Springs, TX 78620
Phone: 833-782-2383
reneeadair@successfulprojects.com
www.successfulprojects.com

# Table of Contents

Introduction ............................................................................................................. 1
**INITIATING** ........................................................................................................ 2
1. Project Selection Methods ............................................................................... 2
2. Feasibility and the Business Case .................................................................... 5
3. High Level Planning .......................................................................................... 7
4. Assign a Project Manager ................................................................................. 8
5. Stakeholder Analysis ...................................................................................... 10
6. Project Charter ............................................................................................... 13
**PLANNING** ...................................................................................................... 14
7. & 8. Scope Statement .................................................................................... 14
9. Divide Large Projects into Phases ................................................................. 18
10. Consult with Subject Matter Experts (SMEs) ............................................. 19
11. Solicit Stakeholders Input ............................................................................ 20
12. Approach Analysis ........................................................................................ 21
13. Create the Work Breakdown Structure (WBS) .......................................... 23
14. Resource Identification Estimating .............................................................. 27
15. Time and Cost Estimating ............................................................................ 28
16. Network Diagramming ................................................................................. 30
17-18. Scheduling and Workload Leveling ........................................................ 38
19. Cost Budgeting ............................................................................................. 45
20. Procurement Plan ......................................................................................... 47
21. Quality Plan ................................................................................................... 48
22. Human Resource Plan .................................................................................. 52
23. Risk Plan ........................................................................................................ 56
24. Change Control Plan .................................................................................... 59
25. Communications Plan ................................................................................... 60
26. Baseline Project Plan .................................................................................... 61
27. Project Plan Approval .................................................................................. 63
**EXECUTING** .................................................................................................... 65
28 Acquire Project Resources .......................................................................... 65
29. Develop Project Team ................................................................................. 66
30. Complete Work Packages ............................................................................ 67
31. Scope Verification ........................................................................................ 68
32. Information Distribution ............................................................................... 69
33. Quality Assurance – Managing Quality ........................................................ 72
34. Procurement Solicitation and Selection ...................................................... 73
**CONTROL & MONITORING** ....................................................................... 74
35. Overall Change Control ............................................................................... 74
36. Scope Control ............................................................................................... 75
37. Performance Reporting ................................................................................ 75
38. Schedule Control .......................................................................................... 77
39. Contract Administration .............................................................................. 78
40. Manage Project Team .................................................................................. 80
41. Manage by Exception to the Project Plan ................................................... 82
42. Quality Control ............................................................................................. 82
43. Risk Monitoring and Control ....................................................................... 84
44. Cost Monitoring & Control ......................................................................... 85
45. Manage Stakeholders – Monitor Engagement ............................................ 88
**CLOSING** ......................................................................................................... 89

46. Procurement Audits ......................................................................................................... 89
47. Product Verification ....................................................................................................... 89
48. Formal Acceptance ......................................................................................................... 89
49. Lessons Learned and Best Practices ............................................................................. 90
50-51. Update Records and Archive Records .................................................................. 95
52. Release Team .................................................................................................................. 95
Glossary of Project Management Terms and Acronyms ................................................ 96
Answer Key ........................................................................................................................ 105
Appendix A – Templates .................................................................................................. 122
Appendix B – Recommended Reading List .................................................................... 123

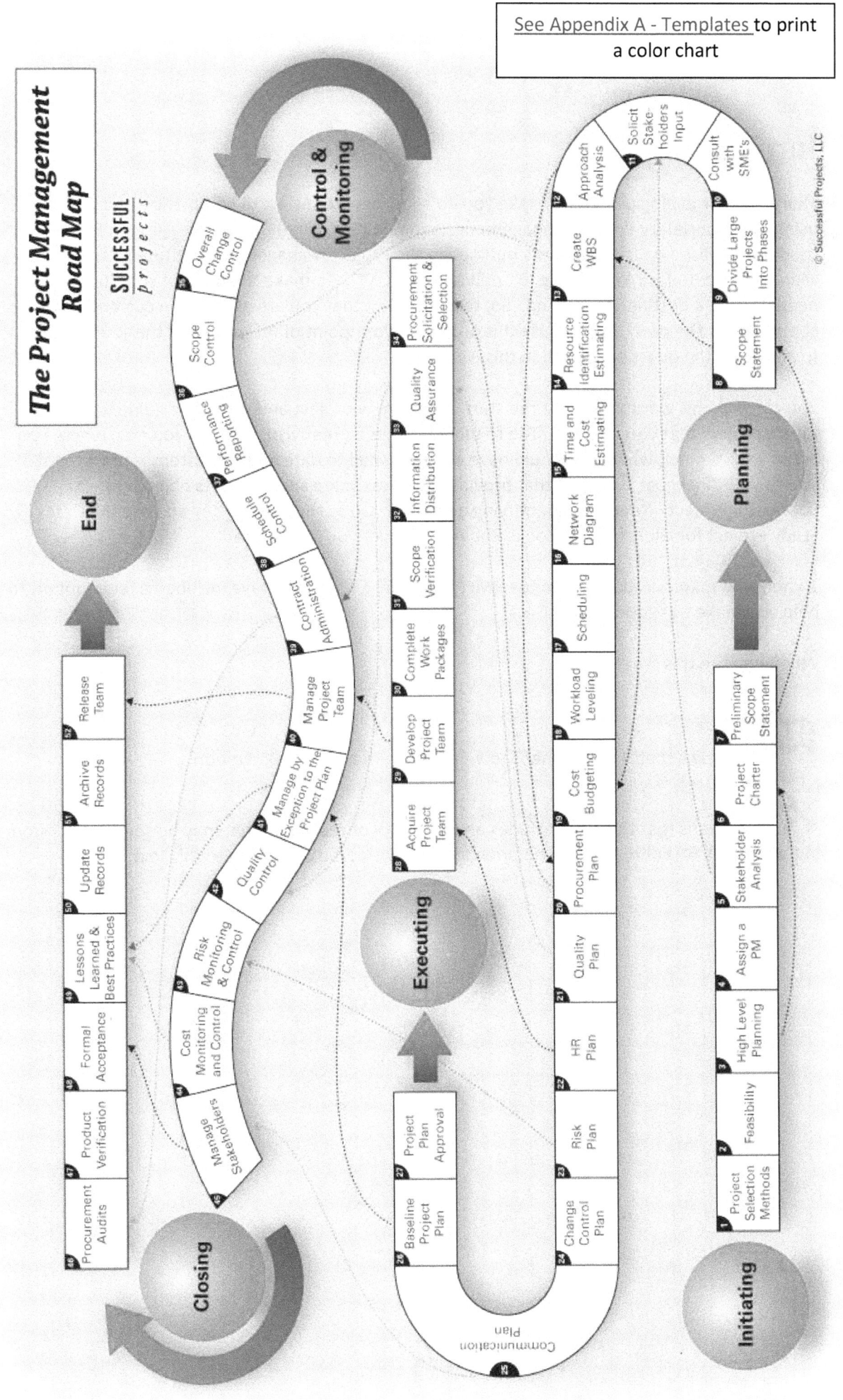

See Appendix A - Templates to print a color chart

# Introduction

Thank you for joining us. We will take you on a journey from start to completion of a project using our proprietary Project Management Roadmap (See Appendix A - Templates). This roadmap is based on the standards outlined in the Project Management Institute's Project Management Body of Knowledge, 6th edition (PMBOK®). To make the most of your journey you need to have a destination in mind. So, take a project that you are working on currently or have completed in the past. You will use this project as your point of reference for this journey and to complete the questions posed in this workbook.

You can pick this workbook up at the start of each new project and use it as a guide for any future project that you manage. The roadmap makes a great visual to help you map where you are in your project, what you should have accomplished to date and what steps remain to take you to your final goal, a project that provides business value and meets its objectives – a Successful Project. Need help identifying a project? Go to the Answer Key and use the Case Study Project for Global Green Books Publishing to get you kick-started.

To help you map our roadmap to the PMI PMBOK 6th Edition, we have included a few symbols to help you make this connection.

When you see this symbol:

 It means that this step maps to a process in the PMBOK 6th Edition

✕ It means that this step includes an *input, tool or technique* that may be specifically listed in the PMBOK 6th Edition or may be provided, as considered beneficial, in this text.

# INITIATING

Initiating your project includes the steps around project selection, definition, and authorization to move forward within your organization.

# 1. Project Selection Methods

Project selection is about determining which projects in the organization's work pipeline are most attractive. In some cases, projects are initiated for compliance or regulatory reasons. A regulatory project may not yield positive financial results but failure to complete it may have a legal and/or a financial impact on the organization or may impact the ability to achieve strategic goals.

Often projects are selected based on financial indicators and anticipated market performance. Projects are generally assessed using some form of economic model. A general knowledge of economic models is necessary as part of a project manager's business acumen.

**Define these in your own words:**

**Time Value of Money** _____

**Opportunity Cost** _____

**Sunk Cost** _____

See Answer Key: 1. Project Selection Methods

**Review these terms:**

*Payback Period* – Time required to recover an initial investment.

*Breakeven Point* – Generally the point in time when cash flow out and cash flow in are equal.

*Present Value* (PV)– Also referred to as Discounted Cash Flow. It is the calculation that is used to determine the potential value of an investment by adjusting the future value (forecasted value) of the investment to the present value. Formula $PV = FV / (1+r)^n$.

*Net Present Value (NPV)* – Used to determine the anticipated dollar value of an investment by summing up the present values for each year of the investment and then subtracting the initial investment. A project with a positive NPV is considered acceptable.

*Return on Investment (ROI)* – Ratio between the net profit and cost of an investment. A higher ROI is favorable.

*Depreciation* – Determining the impact of the effects of time, wear, and the salvage value of capital investments.

*Benefit / Cost Ratio* – Comparing the benefit of an investment with the cost of the investment. Generally, the benefit should be greater than the cost of the investment for a project to be considered acceptable.

## Summary of the Project Selection Formulas

| Present Value | $PV = FV / (1+r)^n$ |
|---|---|
| Future Value | $FV = PV * (1+r)^n$ |
| Net Present Value | NPV = Select biggest number |
| Return on Investment | Net Income/Investment where Net Income = Gross Profit – Expenses; ROI = Select biggest number |
| Payback Period | Add up the projected cash inflow minus expenses until you reach the initial investment. This is also referred to as the breakeven point. |
| Benefit to Cost Ratio | BCR = Benefit / Cost |
| Opportunity cost | The value of the project not selected. |

## Net Present Value (NPV) Sample Problem

Your company is considering the purchase of new machinery to reduce operating costs. The cost to purchase the machine is $90k. Savings will start after 1 year. The cost impacts are projected to be:

| Year | Savings | Factor | Present Value |
|---|---|---|---|
| 0 | -$90k | | |
| 1 | $20k | | |
| 2 | $40k | | |
| 3 | $40k | | |
| 4 | $40k | | |
| 5 | $40k | | |

*Assuming the cost of money is 10%, what would the NPV of this project be?*

## Payback Period Sample Problem:

*A $50k investment is made and earns $35K/year. What is the payback period?*

## Benefit / Cost Ratio Sample Problem:

*A $100k investment is made and earns $40K/year. What is the benefit/cost ratio after 5 years?*

See Answer Key: Net Present Value (NPV) Sample Problem

# Select a Project

For the purposes of the remaining workbook, select a project from your own work or personal experience to use for the exercises. Describe that project below. Need help identifying a project? Go to the Answer Key and use the Case Study Project for Global Green Books Publishing to get you kick-started.

# 2. Feasibility and the Business Case

## Business Case

Projects are undertaken to create business value. Business value is the benefit that the results of the project will bring to its stakeholders. An important input to the start of project planning is business documents including a business case. Creation of business documents generally occurs outside of the project, before it starts.

A business case captures a business problem and contains possible solutions and a recommendation. The business case outlines the *who, what, why, and how* necessary to decide if it is worthwhile continuing a project.

Think of it this way, there is a business requirement (regulatory, cost or time-saving initiative, or a modernization effort) that must be fulfilled. We look at different ways we can accomplish the business requirements, and once we have a list of choices, we narrow these down using criteria that is feasible for that project.

## Feasibility

It is important to explore the feasibility of a project during project selection. You want to explore the viability of an idea. This will help determine whether a project is worth the investment. Consider your project for the following feasibility factors and note your observations in the space below:

1. Is the project technically feasible?
2. Does the project have management support, employee involvement, and commitment?
3. Does the project generate economic benefits?
4. Can the project be financially supported?
5. Can the project be integrated with the local cultural practices and beliefs?
6. Will the project elevate or hinder the participants' social status?
7. Is the project physically and organizationally safe?
8. Is the project politically correct?
9. What is the environmental impact?
10. What is the market demand?
11. What are the expected competitive activities, commercial start-up, and price wars potential?

*Use the space below to explore the feasibility of your project.*

> *If you don't have the time to do it right, when will you have time to do it over?*

# 3. High Level Planning

Planning is an iterative process. As the project evolves, more specific and accurate details are available, the planning gets more detailed. With each successive iteration, the project plan becomes more elaborate and complete. At the beginning of your project, you will be involved in very high-level planning.

## During High Level Planning

1. Think beyond your first approach. Explore thinking small and explore thinking big.

2. Fill in the blank part of the sentence below to help understand the actual completion point of this project:

    *This project will be completed successfully when_____
    is done.*

3. Retrieve previous similar project lessons learned and consider how you will adjust your plan.

4. Plan with an emphasis on suitability, quality, robustness, and effective integration.

5. Consider your project's flexibility profile. Which constraints are most critical to your project?

## Project Flexibility Profile

| Mark the level of flexibility for each constraint | Inflexible<br>Rigid | Adaptable<br>Negotiable | Accepting<br>Can Flex |
|---|---|---|---|
| **Scope/ Quality** | | | |
| **Costs** (HR, financial, and equipment) | | | |
| **Schedule** | | | |

# 4. Assign a Project Manager

As part of the project initiation process and developing the project charter, a project manager will be assigned.

## Consider for Your Project

Name the Project Manager: _____

What **Level of Authority** will the Project Manager be given? *(Select one)*

- ☐ **Project Expeditor**: Acts primarily as a staff assistant and communication coordinator. This role has no authority.

- ☐ **Project Coordinator**: Has some limited, referential authority but still generally serves as a peer to the project team members. However, in addition to his/her hands-on, team-member tasks, this person also has some limited supervisory responsibilities as well as project monitoring and status reporting responsibility.

- ☐ **Project Manager** with very limited authority.

- ☐ **Project Manager** with balanced authority with the Department Managers.

- ☐ **Project Manager** with authority over the Department Managers.

- ☐ **Project Manager** with full authority over all team members.

## Organizational Structure

The project manager's role may be influenced by the organization's structure. Organizational structure refers to the way a company's staff is organized. It is usually defined using a *hierarchal chart* that shows how people report within the organization. A company's organizational structure will affect how resources are allocated to the project and will also influence the role the Project Manager will have within the organization.

Three common organizational structures are Functional, Matrix and Project Oriented. The role of the Project Manager, from a position of power and influence, grows from low to high as you move from Functional to Matrix to Project Oriented.

In a Functional organization, the staff is organized around functions such as IT, Accounting and Engineering. In this structure, resources and those performing the project management role usually report into a Functional or Department Manager. The opposite of the spectrum is the Project-Oriented structure. In this structure, the focus is on the project. Resources are pulled together for the project and report into the Project Manager.

Matrix organizations usually come in three flavors: weak, balanced and strong. Each has progressively more power and influence by the project manager. Often in a weak matrix, the project manager role will be defined but will be more of a project coordinator role. As you move to balanced, the project manager and functional manager have more balanced levels of power and with a strong matrix, there is usually a Project Management Office (PMO) that is providing a level of oversight and the project managers may report into the PMO. With a strong matrix, the project manager has considerable power and influence as it relates to projects.

Consider what type of organizational structure your project will be operating under. Does this impact your role as the project manager?

Consider how this will impact what you include in your project planning documents?

*In the space below, draw an example of a Functional, Balanced Matrix and Project Oriented Hierarchical Organization Chart and indicate where the project manager would fall within each structure.*

See Answer Key: Organizational Structures

# 5. Stakeholder Analysis

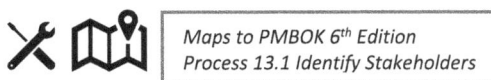

*Maps to PMBOK 6th Edition*
*Process 13.1 Identify Stakeholders*

During stakeholder analysis, you will determine the people, organizations, suppliers, users and anyone else who may be affected by the results of the project. Sometimes it will be obvious who the key stakeholders are, but for more complex projects, a formal analysis is likely to be helpful.

**Stakeholders** – A stakeholder is basically any person or organization either directly involved in or impacted by the project.

Consider who the key stakeholders are for your project (sponsor, customer, project manager, end-user, supplier etc.) as well as other stakeholders who may view your project as a threat or an obstacle to their job position, project or organization (these are negative stakeholders). It is important to determine who the negative stakeholders are and what risks they may introduce during implementation and how they may interrupt the project or prevent the successful completion of your project.

Use the tools on the next page to help you identify all of your project's stakeholders.

> Common stakeholder categories include the following: team members, subject matter experts (SMEs), negative stakeholders, sponsors, project users and vendors.

## Identify Stakeholders

In the figure below, enter your project name in the middle and then brainstorm about all of the potential stakeholders on your project and list them in the bubbles coming out of the center.

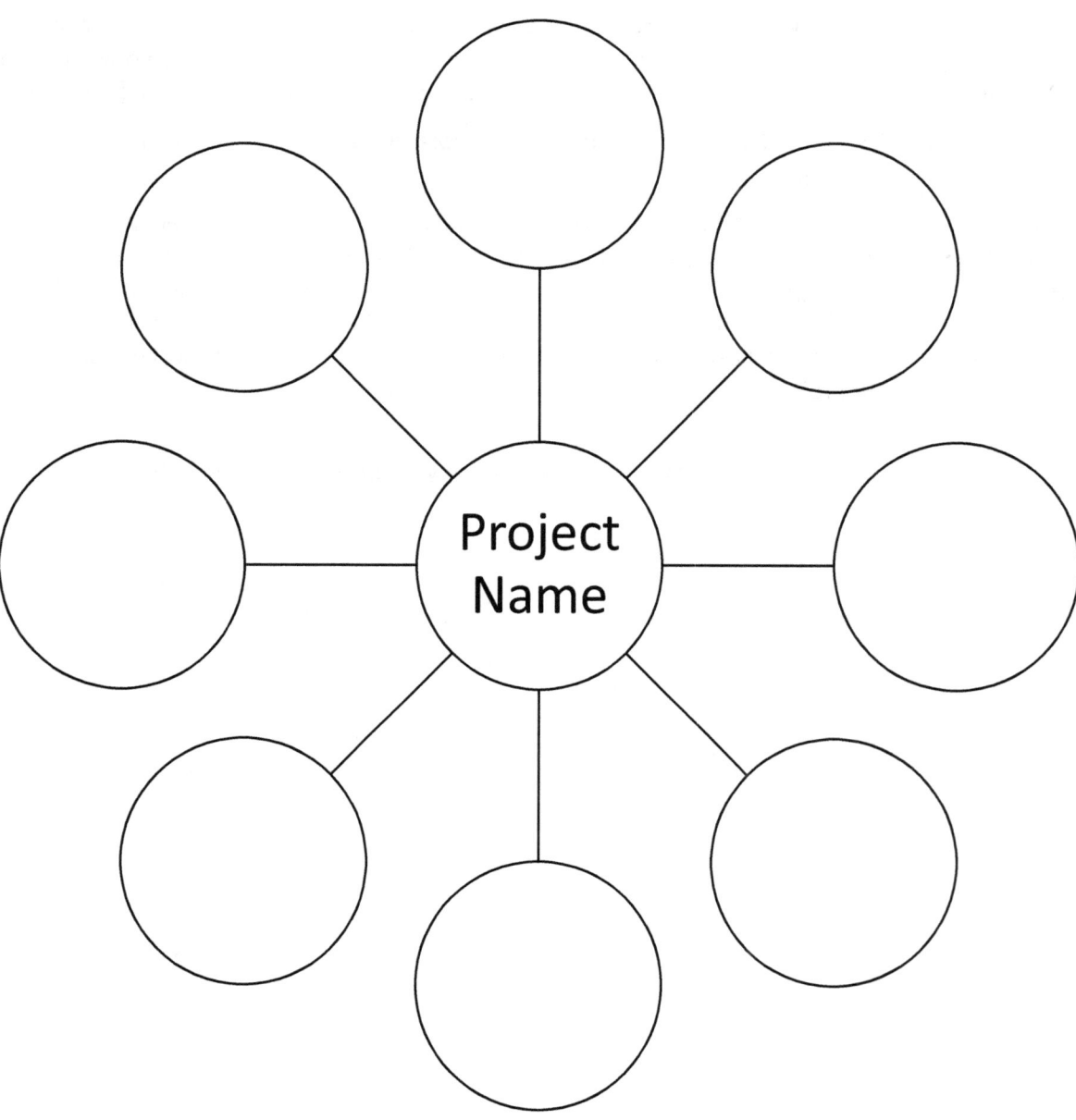

## Stakeholder Power/Influence Grid

The *Power/Interest Grid* is one of the formal approaches project managers use in identifying and managing stakeholders. You can find many examples and variations of this approach on the Internet. Start with the stakeholders you identified and plot the stakeholders in the power/interest grid below based on their level of power and influence on the project. This becomes the basis for your project communication plan.

| Influence & Power | Low Interest | High Interest |
|---|---|---|
| **High** | KEEP SATISFIED | MANAGE CLOSELY |
| **Low** | MONITOR (MINIMUM EFFORT) | KEEP INFORMED |

# 6. Project Charter

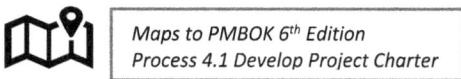

*Maps to PMBOK 6th Edition*
*Process 4.1 Develop Project Charter*

The Project Charter is a simple, yet very powerful document to authorize the project and to empower the project manager. A common technique is to create the Project Charter for your project sponsor, then review it with them and request to have them edit as desired and send it out in their name (aka ghost-writing).

Example of an informal charter e-mail:

---

**To...** All people who may have involvement in the project
**Cc...**
**Subject:** Project X Charter

Project team members in your departments will be responsible for managing their project activities so that they are completed under John Doe's direction within scope, schedule and resource commitments to which we have agreed. It is their responsibility to inform John Doe if they forecast that any of these agreements cannot be met.

Please give John Doe your full cooperation during the planning and completion of this project. Also please forward this email to any people that have not been included on this distribution list that you think may be an interested stakeholder in the project. John Doe will begin by talking with the project stakeholders about their ideas. All interested parties may contact him at jdoe@company.com.

Thanks,

John Doe's Manager

---

See Appendix A - Sample Templates

## Charter Questions

1. Who should send out your project charter?

2. List the points you want to remember to include in your project charter:

3. Suggested distribution list for your charter:

See Answer Key: 6. Project Charter

# PLANNING

Once your project is authorized, you are ready to start formally planning your project. You need to think about all aspects of your project during the planning phase. This includes consideration for defining your scope, schedule, budget and thinking about quality, risk, resources, communications, purchasing needs and managing your stakeholders.

## 7. & 8. Scope Statement

 *Maps to PMBOK 6th Edition Process 5.1 Plan Scope Management*

 *Maps to PMBOK 6th Edition Process 5.3 Define Scope*

 *Maps to PMBOK 6th Edition Process 5.2 Collect Requirements*

Give some thought to defining the project management aspects you will use to validate and control scope throughout your project. This is your Scope Management Plan. For example, what will be your process for preparing the scope statement, your process for creating and then maintaining the WBS, and your process for approving deliverables.

Next is preparing your Scope Statement. Your Scope Statement bridges between Project Initiation and Project Planning.

### Preliminary Scope Statement

During initiation, you may arrive at a Preliminary Project Scope Statement from a review of the Project Charter. At this level, you are only able to address the characteristics and boundaries of the project and its products and services.

### Scope Statement

As you move into project planning and refine your scope, the Scope Statement is crafted and provides detailed information about the project and answers the "Who, What, When, Where, Why" and "How" questions that will clarify the purpose of the project and what work must be completed by the project team.

## What are Your Requirements?

To better understand what needs to be included in your project scope, you need to explore with your stakeholders their specific requirements related to the product or service that will be produced by the project. Take time to document the requirements you gather and make sure they are addressed in your scope and track them to make sure the end result of the project satisfies these original requirements.

Below is a sample Requirements Traceability Matrix.

|   | A | B | C | D | E | F |
|---|---|---|---|---|---|---|
| 1 |   | Important Business Requirement 1 | Important Business Requirement 2 | Important Business Requirement 3 | Important Business Requirement 4 | Important Business Requirement 5 |
| 2 | System Requirement 1 | X |   | X |   |   |
| 3 | System Requirement 2 |   | X |   |   |   |
| 4 | System Requirement 3 |   |   |   |   |   |
| 5 | System Requirement 4 |   | X |   |   |   |
| 6 | System Requirement 5 |   |   | X |   |   |
| 7 | System Requirement 6 |   |   |   | X |   |
| 8 | System Requirement 7 |   |   |   | X |   |
| 9 | System Requirement 8 |   |   |   | X |   |
| 10 | System Requirement 9 |   |   |   | X |   |
| 11 | System Requirement 10 |   |   |   | X |   |
| 12 | System Requirement 11 |   |   |   | X |   |

*What are some of the business requirements of your project?*

**Review These Terms**

**Business Requirements** – These are the high-level business goals of the project/product. Answers the question, "What does the business want to do?" Example: The business needs to actively manage its sales forecast monthly to maximize sales.

**Functional Requirements** – Answers the questions related to how you will meet these business requirements: "What are the features and functionality expected?" "What tools will be used, and what interdependencies are needed?" Example: "The System will create a monthly sales report", "The view sales screen will include an edit button beside each sales order that leads to the edit page for that order."

**User Stories** – A structured way to capture requirements. The structure is "As a (type of user), I want (function) so that (goal)." Example: "As a Sales Executive, I want to see an updated sales forecast monthly so that I can manage the sales funnel."

# Example Scope Statement

**Project Scope Statement**

Project Name: *Computer Upgrade Project*
Originator: *John Smith, CIO*

**Business Purpose:**
*Our 250 stores have a wide variety of computer problems that are difficult to efficiently fix and support. We need to upgrade and standardize the computer systems. Through this project, we can improve overall computer technology, efficiencies, and IT performance.*

**Specific Project Objectives and Goals:**
- *Upgrade Old Technology: Replace the oldest computers to meet minimum technical specifications (to be defined).*
- *Standardization: Reduce the variety of computers and software to a standard list that our IT department can support (to be defined).*
- *To ensure that store equipment is efficiently tested and operating correctly, and that staff is trained and functional on the computers.*

**Project Work Statement:**
*At this time, we are planning to break the project into subprojects to be managed by internal subject matter experts. Sue's department will be in charge of analyzing the software needs, creating specifications, procurement, installation and testing performance at HQ. Bill's department is in charge of the computer setup in the stores, testing on location, and getting operational problems resolved on-site. Mary's department will follow after Bill's team to work on training of the store staff (on location).*

*We are considering alternatives such as waved deployments, centralizing the training, and working with contractors instead of doing so much internally. The approach will likely be redefined during the analysis and planning phase.*

**Key Deliverables:**
- *Needs analysis*
- *Project plan and project management*
- *Hardware and software specifications*
- *Hardware and software procurement*
- *Documentation*
- *Training*
- *Installation and Testing*
- *Support Plan*

**Key Milestones and Schedule Goals:**
- *Project plan presentation by end of Q1*
- *Hardware and software procurement by end of Q2*
- *Installation and testing completed by end of Q3*
- *Training and support set-up completed by end of Q4*

**Major Constraints and Cost Goal:**
- *The project budget is approximately $400,000.*
- *The schedule cannot drag out because computer technology changes fast. If the project gets moved to the back burner, efforts will probably need to start entirely over again.*

**Major Assumptions**
- *We will be eliminating most or all computers that are over 10 years old.*
- *Most computer peripherals will not be affected by this project.*
- *We are moving towards becoming a PC-platform based organization.*
- *HQ and laptop computers are not included in the scope of this project.*

# Exercise: Create Your Project Scope Statement

**Project Scope Statement**

Project Name:
Originator:

**Project Statement:**
*(A quick overview of the project in 15 to 20 words.)*


**Business Purpose:**
*(What are we trying to accomplish?)*


**Specific Project Objectives/Background and Goals:**
*(Reasons for recommending the project, including background information, business problem, and more specific goals.)*


**Project Work Statement**
*(At a high level, what work will you do in this project to deliver the project product? What is the approach you have decided upon?)*


**Key Deliverables**
*(Verifiable outcomes of the work.)*


**Key Milestones and Schedule Goals:**
*(Major events and points in time indicating the progress in implementing your work. Potentially define the phases.)*


**Major Constraints and Cost Goal**
*(Constraints may be physical, technical, resource, or any other limitations.)*


**Major Assumptions**
*(Factors that are not entirely known.)*


See Appendix A – Sample Templates

# 9. Divide Large Projects into Phases

Is your project too large? If so, use this space to break down large projects into a program of smaller projects, or into smaller time-based sub-projects for the sake of better control.

For example, if your project is to install 1,000 computers across the organization. You might create a program for each region (North America, South America) with projects for each office or city within the region. Or, you might decide to roll out a sub-project for PCs and then another sub-project for Apple computers.

Think of your project, can you think of ways to phase your project in?

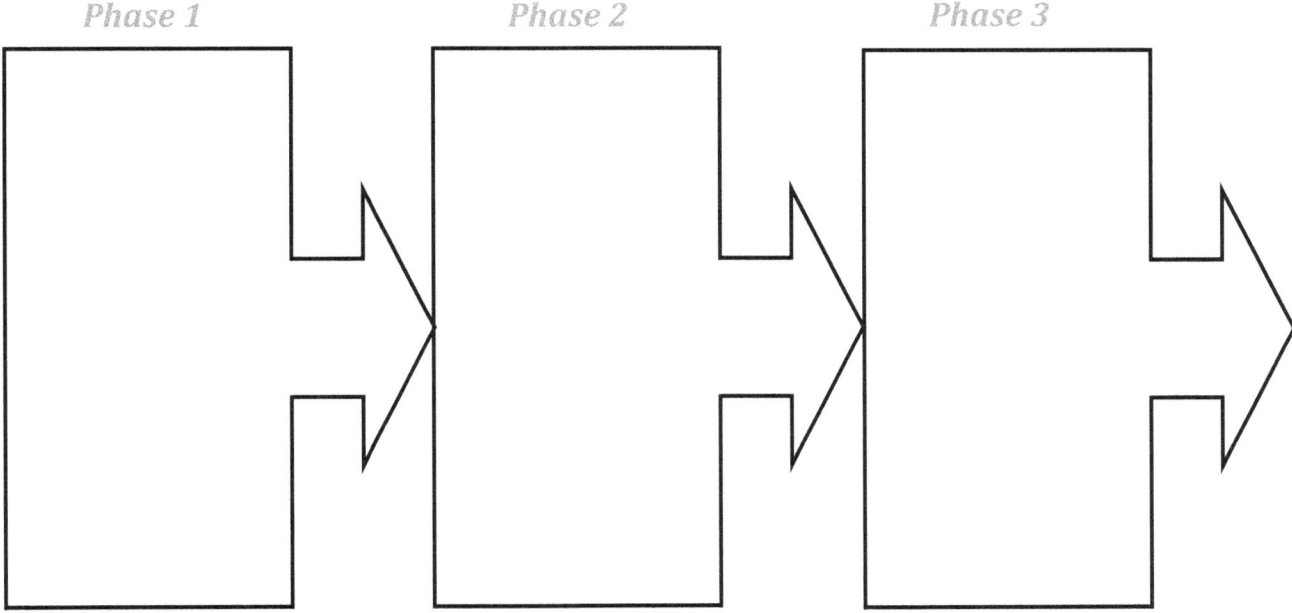

# 10. Consult with Subject Matter Experts (SMEs)

A Subject Matter Expert also referred to as a SME, is a person who has special skills or knowledge on a topic or domain. SMEs should be *interviewed* and consulted regularly throughout your project. Think about your project, who are the SMEs that you will consult?

| Subject | SME Name/Company | Phone | E-mail |
|---------|------------------|-------|--------|
|         |                  |       |        |
|         |                  |       |        |
|         |                  |       |        |
|         |                  |       |        |
|         |                  |       |        |
|         |                  |       |        |
|         |                  |       |        |
|         |                  |       |        |
|         |                  |       |        |
|         |                  |       |        |
|         |                  |       |        |

# 11. Solicit Stakeholders Input

Input from your stakeholders is key during project planning. *Interview* your stakeholders for their input. When soliciting stakeholder input, consider these questions:

1. What improvements would you suggest to the scope or high-level plan?
2. What team members should be involved?
3. Who should have approval responsibilities?
4. Which technologies should be used or avoided?
5. What risks might we encounter?
6. How much should things cost?
7. What do you predict regarding the schedule?
8. What do you suggest for quality specifications?
9. What other stakeholders should be involved?
10. What is the relevance and applicability of the proposed strategies?
11. Are there any gaps and opportunities for action?
12. What criteria should be used for prioritizing strategies?

# 12. Approach Analysis

*Alternative Analysis* is a technique used to evaluate various options to determine which approach to use in your project.

For example, consider how you will approach sourcing materials and people or what your project oversight approach will be. Are you making assumptions related to the chosen approach?

## Make or Buy Decisions

As part of project planning, you will need to consider what you are going to make, or take care of internally, versus what you will hire out or purchase. Conduct this analysis for your project in the space below.

| Make/Do Inside Organization | Hire Out or Purchase |
|---|---|
|  |  |
|  |  |
|  |  |
|  |  |
|  |  |

## Understanding Your Unique Project Rules

Otherwise known as project governance, project rules spell out the framework within which project decisions are made. Project governance is a critical element of any project. Accountabilities and responsibilities associated with an organization's business as usual activities are often outlined in organizational processes, procedures, and organizational charts. There is seldom an equivalent framework that exists to govern projects.

For example, the organization chart provides a good indication of who in the organization is responsible for any particular operational activity the organization conducts. But unless an organization has specifically developed a project governance policy, no such chart is likely to exist for project activity.

Validate Critical Data

**Consider:**

- ☐ What percent of team member work time (or average hours per work day) will be dedicated to this project?
- ☐ What organizational or industry methodologies will be used?
- ☐ How will the project be funded?
- ☐ Will there be regularly scheduled meetings or just "as-needed" meetings?
- ☐ Will the project team be co-located or virtual?
- ☐ Determine the project escalation procedures.
    - ○ What will the project thresholds be? Who will be notified if they are hit?
    - ○ Who will the customer or team members notify if the project manager is not satisfying them?

## Project Assumptions

An assumption is a belief of what you assume to be true. You make assumptions based on your knowledge, experience or the information available on hand. Assumptions are anticipated events or circumstances that are expected to occur during your project's life cycle.

Assumptions are supposed to be true but do not necessarily end up being true. Sometimes they may turn out to be false, which can affect your project significantly. Assumptions add risks to the project because they may or may not be true.

**So, what project assumptions have not yet been validated for your project?**

| Assumption | Assigned Person | Date Validated | Determined True/False |
|---|---|---|---|
|  |  |  |  |
|  |  |  |  |
|  |  |  |  |
|  |  |  |  |
|  |  |  |  |
|  |  |  |  |
|  |  |  |  |
|  |  |  |  |
|  |  |  |  |
|  |  |  |  |
|  |  |  |  |
|  |  |  |  |
|  |  |  |  |

# 13. Create the Work Breakdown Structure (WBS)

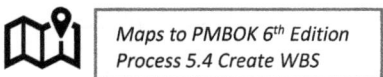 Maps to PMBOK 6th Edition Process 5.4 Create WBS

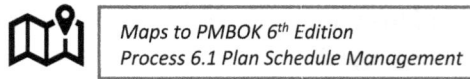 Maps to PMBOK 6th Edition Process 6.1 Plan Schedule Management

The WBS breaks the project down into smaller more manageable components and allows for more effective and reliable time and cost estimating. WBS development produces a hierarchical grouping of project components and tasks and *is not intended to display the sequence of tasks and activities.*

WBS templates will accelerate the process and may be developed by using previous projects. A PMO may develop standard WBS templates for use during project planning.

**What are the benefits associated with developing and using a Work Breakdown Structure?**




See Answer Key: 13. Create the Work Breakdown Structure (WBS)

**Consider the Following Checklist as you Create Your WBS**
- ☐ The WBS has been written to account for every aspect of the project work.
- ☐ The project team participated in building the WBS or has reviewed and approved it.
- ☐ Project management work is included in the WBS.
- ☐ Work packages have been broken down to a level that can be delegated, but not so far as to be micromanaging.

# Example WBS for a Web Project

1. Website Redesign for XYZ Company
    1.1. Planning/Project Definition
        1.1.1. High-level plan
        1.1.2. Assign a PM
        1.1.3. Stakeholder Analysis
        1.1.4. Project Charter
        1.1.5. Project Scope Statement
        1.1.6. Divide Large Web Site Project into Phases or Smaller Projects
        1.1.7. Consult with SMEs
        1.1.8. Solicit Stakeholder Input
        1.1.9. Approach Analysis
            1.1.9.1. Technical Approach
                1.1.9.1.1. System Requirements
                1.1.9.1.2. Business Requirements
                1.1.9.1.3. Web Design Methods Evaluation
            1.1.9.2. Determination of What to Do Internally and What to Hire out
    1.2. Conceptual Design Development
        1.2.1. Business Logic Design
        1.2.2. User Interface Design
            1.2.2.1. Artist Design Concepts – Alternative Creative Treatments
            1.2.2.2. Graphical Treatment Feedback
            1.2.2.3. Graphical Design Draft #2
            1.2.2.4. Graphical Design - Final
        1.2.3. Internal Design Standards Consultation
        1.2.4. Industry Design Standards Consultation
    1.3. Construction
        1.3.1. Staging/Development Server Set-Up
        1.3.2. Production Server Set-Up
        1.3.3. Graphical Asset Placement
            1.3.3.1. Graphical Splitting & Optimization
            1.3.3.2. Template Structure/Coding
        1.3.4. Navigation
        1.3.5. Special feature coding
            1.3.5.1. Flash
            1.3.5.2. Widgets
            1.3.5.3. Video
        1.3.6. Application Programming
        1.3.7. Content Population
    1.4. Testing
        1.4.1. Test Plan Development
        1.4.2. Testing Execution
        1.4.3. Analyze Defects/Correct
        1.4.4. Production Readiness Verification/Approval
    1.5. Deployment
        1.5.1. Files Transferred
        1.5.2. Retest
        1.5.3. Analyze Defects/Correct
        1.5.4. Domain redirected to new site
    1.6. Search Engine Optimization (SEO)
        1.6.1. Written text optimization
        1.6.2. Meta tag entries
        1.6.3. Search Engines Seeded
        1.6.4. Ranking Monitor/Report
    1.7. Marketing/Announcements
    1.8. Content Management Training
    1.9. Project Closure

See Appendix A - Templates

## Plan for Your Project WBS

Create your WBS Levels 1-2. Start by brainstorming your WBS organization within the space below. Then use the following page to begin to decompose your WBS.

*Blank page to continue your WBS*

The WBS you create is the cornerstone of your planning effort. All of your planning activities build on this foundational structure. After you have the WBS in place, you can begin to progressively elaborate the work packages by defining the specific activities required to complete each work package and outline the sequencing of the various activities.

Also, take some time to think through if there are any rules or assumptions that will go into your schedule development such as using days or weeks as your unit of measure or assuming a US Holiday schedule for your calendar. These decisions will make up your Schedule Management Plan.

# 14. Resource Identification Estimating

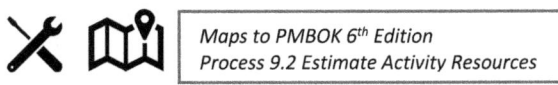
*Maps to PMBOK 6th Edition*
*Process 9.2 Estimate Activity Resources*

List the people, equipment, and materials that are expected to be needed for the project. The outcome of resource identification is often a printed **Resource Breakdown Structure (RBS)**. If you structure your WBS by organizational departments this is called an **Organizational Breakdown Structure (OBS).** Explore these concepts further through Internet searches on these terms.

| People/Skills | Equipment | Materials |
|---|---|---|
| | | |
| | | |
| | | |
| | | |
| | | |
| | | |
| | | |
| | | |
| | | |
| | | |

# 15. Time and Cost Estimating

 *Maps to PMBOK 6th Edition Process 6.4 Estimate Activity Durations*

 *Maps to PMBOK 6th Edition Process 7.1 Plan Cost Management*

 *Maps to PMBOK 6th Edition Process 7.2 Estimate Costs*

After you have the WBS outlined and resources identified, you need to estimate the time and cost required for each work package. Below are some best practices to consider as you estimate.

## Estimating Best Practices

**Compare actuals to estimates**
After the work is complete, compare the actual time the work took to the original estimate. Track the percent off (either under or over) and report that information back to the team members. The best way to improve estimating accuracy is by paying attention. The best way to pay attention is by tracking metrics.

**Use more than one approach or more than one person, or both.**
After you have one estimate, compare the logic using either another approach or another person's perspective.

**Clearly write out what makes this work complete.**
Many times, there are unknown needed revisions, quality acceptance criteria, and a level of completeness that has not been clearly thought out, not to mention communicated to the person doing the estimating.

**Present estimates in either a range or by indicating your level of confidence.**
For example, our project team estimates this will cost $100,000, and we have a confidence level of -20% to +60% (meaning it could very possibly fall between $80,000 and $160,000).

**Understand the definition of an estimate.**
In many knowledge projects (such as engineering, research, IT, creative, and etc.) the time work takes to create unique deliverables can be extremely difficult to accurately estimate. And eventually, the estimation discussion turns into a risk tolerance question. It generally needs to be agreed that without seriously inflating estimates to turn them into guarantees, that schedules are best planned with some flexibility and contingency for going over. There are diminishing returns in over-analyzing the project.

**Ask SMEs.**
Subject matter experts can be a big help, especially in informing project managers what the commonly overlooked work or costs are. There are very common estimation omissions. You will benefit from questioning what they are.

Use the space below to consider your WBS created in Step 13. Think of the approaches you would use to arrive at estimates for each activity.

> The same work under the same conditions will be estimated differently by ten different estimators or by one estimator at ten different times.

# 16. Network Diagramming

  *Maps to PMBOK 6th Edition Process 6.2 Define Activities*  *Maps to PMBOK 6th Edition Process 6.3 Sequence Activities*

As a project manager, it is important to setup a logical relationship among the activities in your WBS so that everyone understands the sequence of the activities in the project and any dependencies among the activities so that they can work in an ideal manner to accomplish the project goals.

A network diagram is a graphical representation of the project and is composed of a series of connected arrows and boxes to describe the inter-relationship between the activities involved in the project. Boxes or nodes represent the description of activities and arrows show the relationship between the activities. There must be a start and finish activity and all the other activities fall within these two. The most common way to develop the network diagram is using the *precedence diagramming method (PDM)*.

We are going to have you go through creating a few network diagrams. Review the instructions below as you complete the exercises on the following pages. Often, you will use a software product to create your project schedule which automates this process for you. However, it is still important to understand how this is calculated.

## Calculation Instructions

1. Flowchart the activities in the order that the work needs to be done.
    a. Put the Task Names or IDs in the boxes and draw dependencies with arrows
    b. Insert the Duration Estimate for each box. You may use any time units (such as hours, days, weeks, months, or years), but remember to be consistent by using the same unit of measurement throughout the project. The most common choice is business days.
2. Calculate the forward pass to determine the early start and finish for the work.
    a. Put 1 in the Early Start for the work that can begin at the start.
    b. Add the Early Start number to the Duration number. Then subtract one. That becomes the Early Finish number of the first task.
    c. Add one to the Early Finish from that task and put it into the Early Start of the tasks coming off that box.
    d. When faced with a sink point (aka convergent point), the Early Start that we choose is the largest of the Early Finish numbers from the preceding boxes.
3. Calculate the backward pass from right to left. This fills in the Late Start and Late Finish for each task. Below are step-by-step instructions for helping to do that:

a. Begin the backward pass at the end of the project. Take the number in the Early Finish of the Last Task, or in the end marker, and put it into the Late Finish of the same task.
b. From the Late Finish, subtract the task duration and add one to get the number for the Late Start. Remember you are working from right to left now.
c. As you move left in the tasks, subtract one from the early start task to fill in the late start of connected tasks.
d. When you have multiple choices, the Late Start that carries to the predecessors Late Finish is the smallest number of the options.
e. Calculate the Slack/Float for each task. The value of the Slack/Float is calculated as the difference between the Early Start and the Late Start.

4. Find the critical path and mark it in red. The critical path is the longest path through the project schedule. All activities on the critical path have 0 slack.

## Common Types of Dependency Relationships
Listed from most to least common

- **Finish-to-Start:** The task to the left must be completed before the task to the right can start. This is by far the most commonly used dependency relationship in network diagrams, accounting for over 90% of most dependency relationships.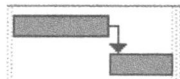

- **Finish-to-Finish:** The second task cannot finish until the first task finishes. For example, "Inspect Electrical" cannot finish until "Add wiring" finishes.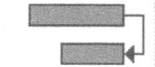

- **Start-to-Start**: The second task cannot start until the first task starts. For example, if you "Pour foundation" first, you can and should begin the process to "Level Concrete".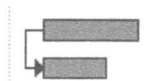

## Common Types of Imposed Dates

- **Fixed Early Start**: A task's early start date is set to the imposed date. It does not affect the tasks late date calculations.
- **Fixed Early Finish**: A task's early finish is set to the imposed date. It does not affect the tasks late date calculations.
- **Fixed Late Start**: A task's late start is set to the imposed date. It does not affect the tasks early date calculations.
- **Fixed Late Finish**: A task must finish on the imposed date. It does not affect the early date calculations.
- **Start Not Earlier Than**: A task cannot finish earlier than the imposed date. This has implications on late start-finish dates.
- **Start Not Later Than**: A task cannot start later than the imposed date. This has implications on early start-finish dates.
- **Finish Not Later Than**: A task cannot finish later than the imposed date. This has implications on early start-finish dates with the potential for float.
- **Must Start On**: Customer or organization-imposed start date; driven by project start.
- **Must Finish On**: Customer or organization-imposed finish date; potential for negative float.
- **Work Between**: Must work between two imposed dates; potential for negative float.

> *Hard logic is an activity relationship based on technical needs (i.e.: the software must arrive before we can install it on our server). Soft logic is a preference to do work in a certain order that may be based on team member time, available skills, or other reasoning that may have flexibility.*

## Network Calculation Exercises
Let's try a few easy network diagrams.

### Very Easy

| Early Start | Duration | Early Finish |
|---|---|---|
| Task Name or ID ||| 
| Late Start | Slack | Late Finish |

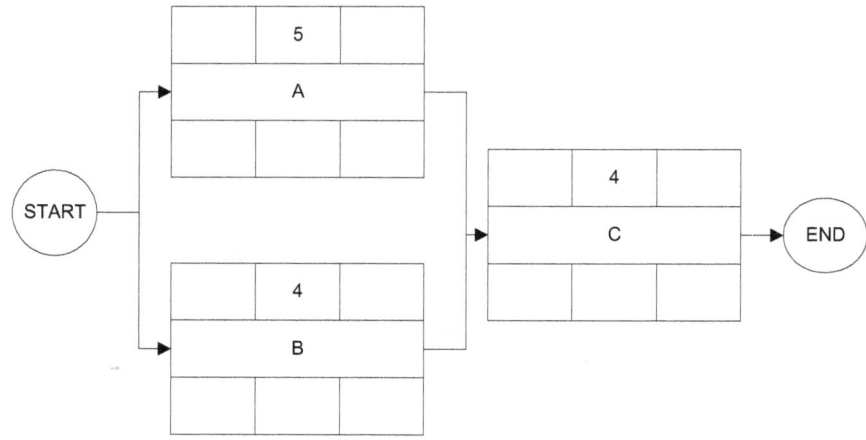

### Easy

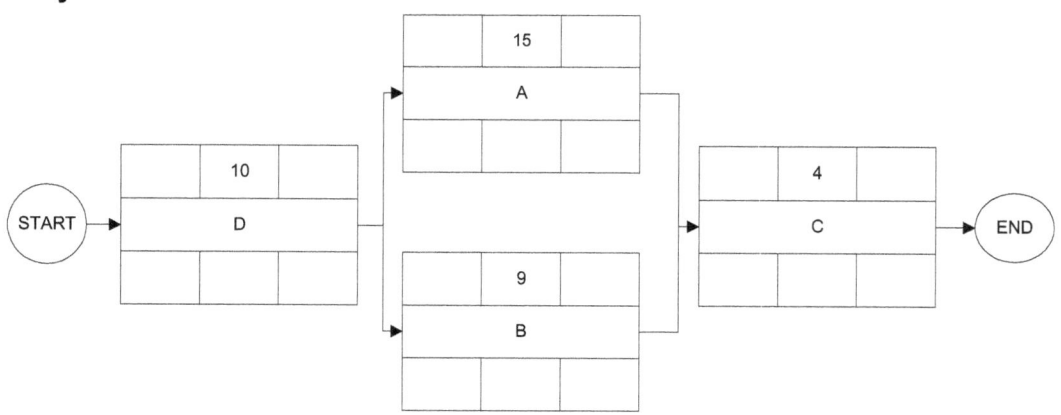

See Answer Key: 16. Network Diagramming: Network Calculation Exercises

Now let's try a few harder ones. These are optional so if you are struggling with this concept, work towards mastery of the concepts with the very easy and easy examples.

**Moderate**

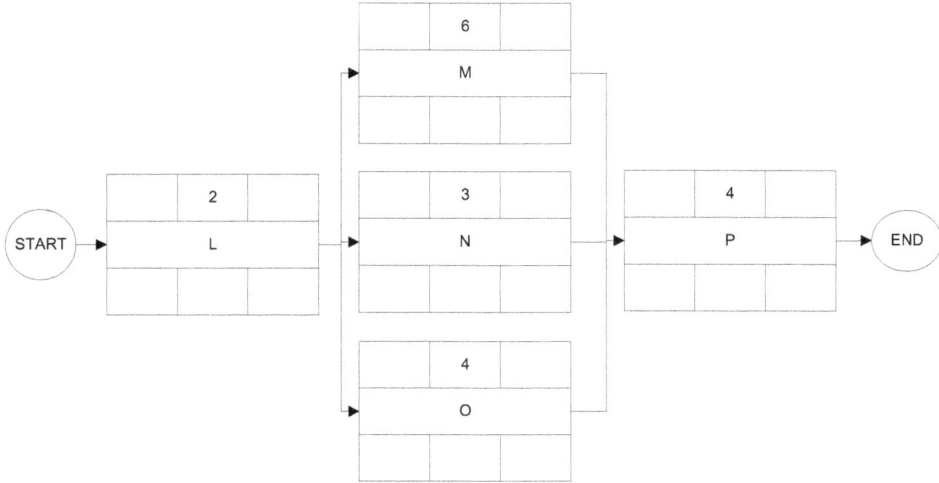

**Difficult**

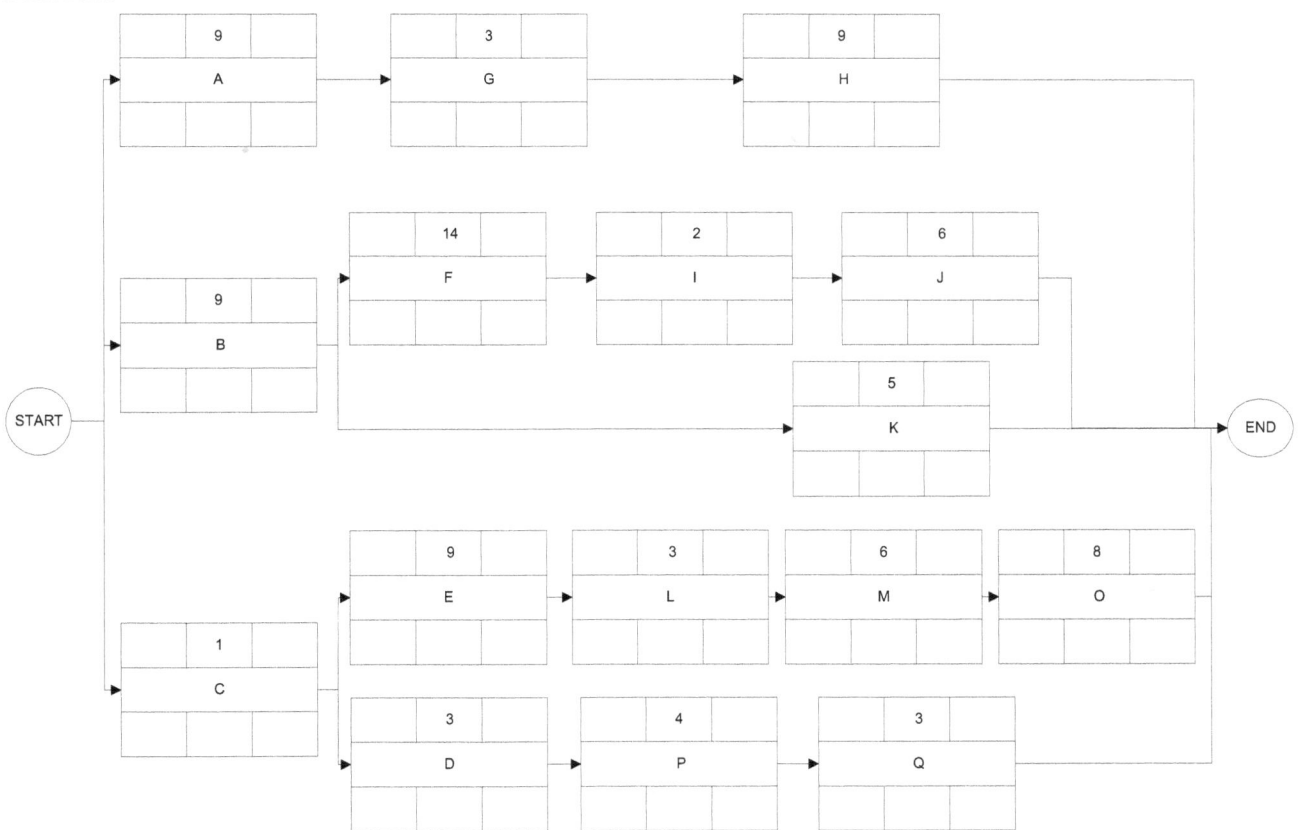

See Answer Key: **Moderate**

# Network Diagrams to Calculate from Tables

You may see information to build your network diagram provided in a table format. Draw out your network diagram from the information provided below. What is your critical path? What is the duration of the project?

## Project A

| Project A | | |
|---|---|---|
| Work Package | Duration | Dependent Upon/Relationship/Lag |
| A | 5 weeks | Start |
| B | 3 weeks | A, F-S |
| C | 6 weeks | A, F-S, -1 |
| D | 2 weeks | B, S-S, + 3 |
| E | 7 weeks | D, F-S |
| F | 5 weeks | C, F-S, -2 |
| G | 8 weeks | F, S-S, +1 |
| H | 2 weeks | F, F-S, +3 |
| I | 4 weeks | H, F-S, -1 |

<u>See Answer Key:</u> *Network Diagrams to Calculate from Tables:*

Try another practice with many leads and lags and a start-to-start relationship below:

# Project B

| Work Package | Project B Duration | Dependent Upon/Relationship/Lag |
|---|---|---|
| A | 5 weeks | Start |
| B | 3 weeks | Start |
| C | 6 weeks | B, S-S |
| D | 2 weeks | C, F-S, + 5 |
| E | 7 weeks | D, F-S, -1 |
| F | 5 weeks | C, F-S, +3 |
| G | 8 weeks | F, F-S, +10 |
| H | 2 weeks | E, F-S, +3 |
| I | 4 weeks | C, F-S, +12 |

See Answer Key: Project B

By now you should be getting the idea. Try another project with another S-S relationship below:

## Project C

| Work Package | Project C Duration | Dependent Upon/Relationship/Lag |
|---|---|---|
| A | 15 weeks | Start |
| B | 13 weeks | A, F-S |
| C | 16 weeks | B, F-S |
| D | 12 weeks | C, F-S, + 5 |
| E | 17 weeks | D, S-S, -1 |
| F | 15 weeks | C, F-S |

See Answer Key: Project C

# 17-18. Scheduling and Workload Leveling

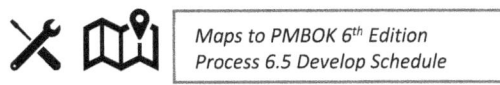

*Maps to PMBOK 6th Edition*
*Process 6.5 Develop Schedule*

After you have your idealized network diagram, you will need to negotiate the workload leveled work dates with your project team and develop your project schedule. Start with your project network diagram to meet with your team members and their department managers. Perform the workload leveling and schedule the work as actual appointments for the upcoming 3 months. For the remainder of the project schedule, it is normal to plan around milestone dates.

## Resource Optimization

Resource optimization is a method of gaining efficiency and consistency of resource utilization within the project. Resources should not be over-allocated at any given time period within their calendar availability. *Resource Leveling* and *Resource Smoothing* are resource optimization techniques which are used to adjust the project schedule due to the demand and supply issues of project resources.

**Can You Define These Terms Related to Resource Optimization?**

**Resource Leveling**



**Resource Smoothing**



See Answer Key: 17-18. Scheduling and Workload Leveling

## Schedule Compression

Schedule compression is a technique used to shorten an already developed schedule. This might be done to meet a particular delivery date or accommodate a new opportunity or schedule delay. It's done without changing the scope of the program. There are two techniques that are commonly used are *Crashing* and *Fast Tracking*.

### Can You Define These Terms Relate to Schedule Compression?

**Crashing**

**Fast Tracking**

See Answer Key: 17-18. Scheduling and Workload Leveling

## Practice Problem: Determining Mark's Project Work Completion

*You are a project manager trying to determine the date one of your team members, Mark can be done with his part of your project work. In preparation for doing this, you have already talked with Mark to discuss his part of the project deliverables, the dependency of the order of work, and his estimated time to complete his 7 tasks. Mark has informed you that although he has other work as well, he can devote 6 hours a day to this project except for on the first two days – when he can only devote 3 hours a day to the project.*

*The tasks that Mark's work is dependent upon should be completed in time so that Mark can start his part on the first day of a month that coincidentally also falls on a Monday. Mark estimates his 7 tasks will each take 6 hours, totaling 42 work hours. The 7 tasks all have finish-to-start dependency relationships.*

*There is a lag of 3 work days between tasks 2 & 3 for inspection and approval of task 2 (which is expected to go well). Saturdays and Sundays are non-working days and Mark is on vacation on the 12th. When will Mark be complete with his part of the project? You may use the table below to help you in your schedule planning.*

| # Day | 1 | 2 | 3 | 4 | 5 | 6 | 7 | 8 | 9 | 10 | 11 | 12 | 13 | 14 | 15 | 16 | 17 | 18 | 19 | 20 |
|---|---|---|---|---|---|---|---|---|---|---|---|---|---|---|---|---|---|---|---|---|
| Day of Week | Mon | Tues | Wed | Thur | Fri | Sat | Sun | Mon | Tues | Wed | Thur | Fri | Sat | Sun | Mon | Tues | Wed | Thur | Fri | Sat |
| | | | | | | | | | | | | | | | | | | | | |
| | | | | | | | | | | | | | | | | | | | | |

See Answer Key: Practice Problem: Determining Mark's Project Work Completion

# Yearly Calendar

Use this 3-year calendar to help plan the dates associated with your project schedule.

*[3-year calendar image for 2018, 2019, and 2020 with federal holidays listed for each year]*

## Making Smart Project Schedule Decisions

Let's bring it all together in a more difficult problem. Build a network diagram based on the project information below.

| Activity Name | Preceding Activity (Assume all are finish-to-start relationships) | Time (weeks) | Planned Value | Assigned Team |
|---|---|---|---|---|
| A | - | 7 | $1,000 | Fred |
| B | - | 8 | $22,000 | Mary |
| C | - | 6 | $3,000 | Jane & Team |
| D | A | 6 | $5,000 | Fred |
| E | B | 6 | $11,000 | Mary |
| F | B | 8 | $1,000 | Jane & Team |
| G | C | 4 | $5,000 | Jane & Team |
| H | D, E | 7 | $10,000 | Fred |
| I | F, G, H | 3 | $1,000 | Jane & Team |
| J | I | 3 | $5,000 | Fred |
| K | I | 2 | $1,000 | Mary |
| L | I | 5 | $10,000 | Jane & Team |

From the information above, create a network diagram and determine how long the project will take if the estimated durations are correct?

1. What activities create the project's critical path?

2. What is G's slack time if C used 6 weeks of its available slack time?

3. During week 1 what activity is your greatest concern?

4. If Jane and her Team can't do any work on this project during weeks 9 and 10, can we still work with them and achieve our schedule?

5. If you had to pick 4 milestone points in the project based on the network diagram, where would they fall?

6. Assume you are the project manager and you want to take a 2-week vacation sometime during the project. When is the best time for you to be out on vacation? Does a network diagram or Gantt chart do a better job of helping you make this decision?

7. Create a line chart of the cumulative planned project expenditures assuming work happens as soon as possible, and that billing is done upon completion of the activities.

8. Compare and contrast the usefulness of the network diagram, Gantt chart, and line chart of expenditures.

9. If the customer wants the project schedule shortened, what is the best activity to focus on shortening (crashing)? The second and third best? Remember that it only pays to crash the work that is on the critical path because the other work already has float/slack time available.

10. Assuming the crash table information in the table that follows to be correct, what are the best crash priorities based purely on cost?

See Answer Key: Making Smart Project Schedule Decisions

## Crash Table

To determine which tasks to crash you only need to look at the tasks on the critical path. Find the incremental cost increase by subtracting the current cost from compressed cost and then dividing that by the compressed duration to arrive at the weekly cost to compress. You would then prioritize these by the lowest cost to highest cost.

| Task | Current | | Compressed | | Weekly cost to compress (crash cost) | Crash priority |
|---|---|---|---|---|---|---|
| | Duration | Cost | Duration | Cost | | |
| A | 7 | $1,000 | 3 | $5,000 | | |
| B | 8 | $22,000 | 4 | $30,000 | | |
| C | 6 | $3,000 | 5 | $4,000 | | |
| D | 6 | $5,000 | 6 | $5,000 | | |
| E | 6 | $11,000 | 4 | $17,000 | | |
| F | 8 | $1,000 | 7 | $2,000 | | |
| G | 4 | $5,000 | 2 | $8,000 | | |
| H | 7 | $10,000 | 3 | $25,000 | | |
| I | 3 | $1,000 | 2 | $2,000 | | |
| J | 3 | $5,000 | 2 | $6,000 | | |
| K | 2 | $1,000 | 1 | $1,500 | | |
| L | 5 | $10,000 | 2 | $16,000 | | |

See Answer Key: Crash Table

# Gantt Charts

*Gantt charts* tend to be the favorite schedule view for many senior executives. They are easy to comprehend and can show the completed work (usually indicated by showing a line through the bar).

The disadvantage of a Gantt chart, as compared to a network diagram, can be the difficulty in seeing the critical path, dependency relationships, and slack time. However, this information may be of more importance to the project manager than the executive level sponsors.

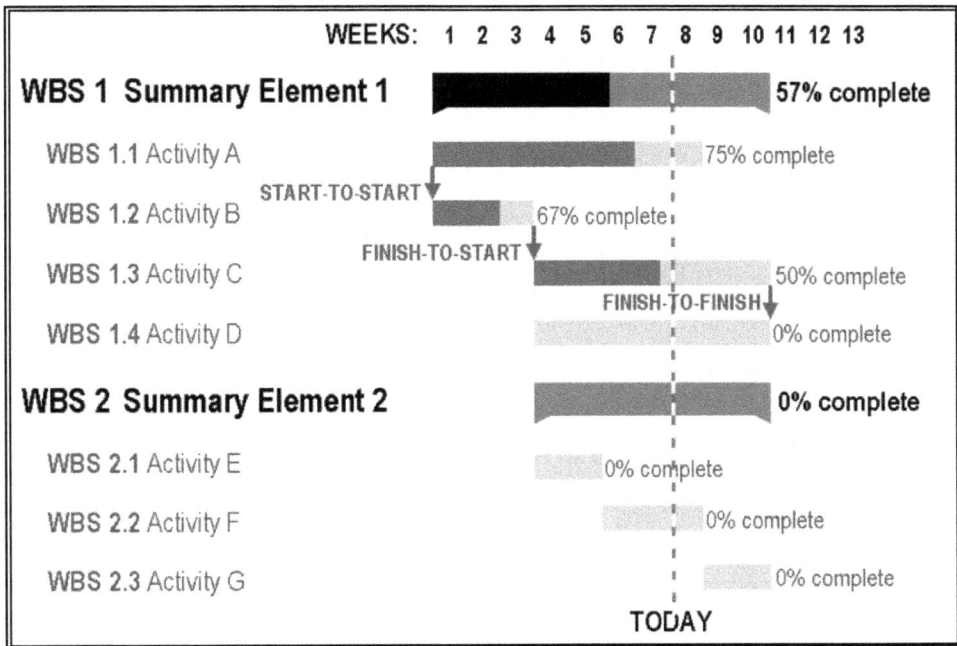

1: Another style of Gantt chart. Source: Garry L. Booker, Rights released to public domain. Oct. 8, 2007.

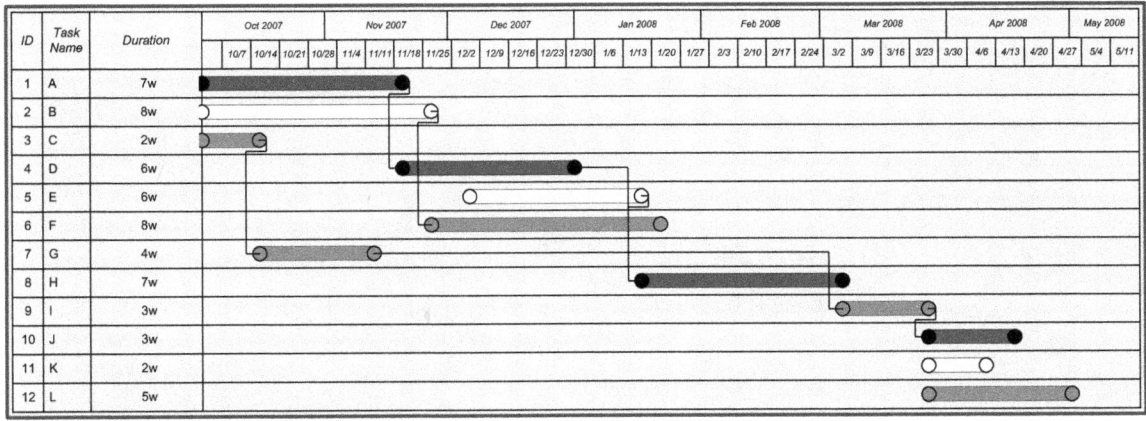

2: Gantt chart example produced in MS Visio

# 19. Cost Budgeting

 *Maps to PMBOK 6th Edition Process 7.1 Plan Cost Management*   *Maps to PMBOK 6th Edition Process 7.3 Determine Budget*

Initially, the Project Budget allows the project manager to determine how much the project is likely to cost. Throughout the course of the project, it lets the project manager check whether or not the project is sticking to its budget. The cost budget is generally the sponsor-approved total cost baseline of a project. This often includes the estimated costs (Step 15) plus any approved project contingency and management reserves.

When developing your budget and preparing to track progress, think through your cost management approach and any rules, such as using US Dollars, if you will use rounding or that the budget will be maintained in Excel. This is your Cost Management Plan.

$$\begin{aligned}&\text{Sum of Costs of Work packages}\\&+\text{Total Project Cost Contingency/Reserves}\\&+\underline{\text{Management Contingency/Reserves}}\\&=\text{Total Project Budget}\end{aligned}$$

**Review these Terms**

**Project Contingency:** Contingencies are also called buffers, reserves, or padding. They are the funds or time needed above the initial estimate to reduce the risk to an acceptable level. It is important to include contingencies in the project estimates.

**Management Reserve**: A financial or schedule reserve, or buffer, that is available to the project, but that the project manager must get permission to utilize. This reserve is for "unknown unknowns" unlike the project contingency, which is for "known unknowns".

Use a budget template, along with your WBS, and create a budget for your project. Below is a sample of what data points might be included.

| WBS | Task | Labor | | Materials | | Fixed Costs | Budget | Actual | Under(Over) |
|---|---|---|---|---|---|---|---|---|---|
| | | Hrs | Rate | Units | $/Unit | | | | |
| 1 | [ Level 1 Category ] | | | | | | $ 1,000.00 | $ 555.00 | $ 445.00 |
| 1.1 | [ Level 2 Task ] | 8.0 | $22.50 | 25.0 | $4.50 | $50.00 | 600.00 | 342.50 | 257.50 |
| 1.2 | [ Level 2 Task ] | 10.0 | $21.25 | | | $212.50 | 400.00 | 212.50 | 187.50 |
| 2 | [ Level 1 Category ] | | | | | | $ - | $ - | $ - |
| 2.1 | [ Level 2 Task ] | | | | | | | | |
| 2.2 | [ Level 2 Task ] | | | | | | | | |
| | | | | | | | | | |

See Appendix A – Sample Templates

Use the space below to create your project budget.

| WBS | Task | Labor | | Materials | | Fixed Costs | Budget | Actual | Under(Over) |
|---|---|---|---|---|---|---|---|---|---|
| | | Hrs | Rate | Units | $/Unit | | | | |
| | | | | | | | | | |
| | | | | | | | | | |
| | | | | | | | | | |
| | | | | | | | | | |
| | | | | | | | | | |
| | | | | | | | | | |
| | | | | | | | | | |
| | | | | | | | | | |
| | | | | | | | | | |
| | | | | | | | | | |
| | | | | | | | | | |
| | | | | | | | | | |
| | | | | | | | | | |
| | | | | | | | | | |
| | | | | | | | | | |
| | | | | | | | | | |
| | | | | | | | | | |

# 20. Procurement Plan

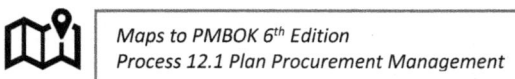

*Maps to PMBOK 6th Edition*
*Process 12.1 Plan Procurement Management*

Often, you will need to make decisions related to procurement planning. These decisions involve which items will be internally procured and which items will be externally outsourced or purchased. This information can heavily impact the project's budget.

During procurement planning, you may need to create sample procurement documents and develop selection criteria to help with the selection process of potential vendors. The selection process will involve comparing and contrasting vendors' advantages, disadvantages, and contractual offerings and awarding procurement contracts.

You will also need to consider how the contracts will be administered. For example, which tools and processes will be used to manage relationships with vendors. During project execution, procurement activities may drive project changes that will need to be tracked. A centralized system of contract change monitoring and control should be used to evaluate and determine whether potential changes to contracts are needed.

**For your project, consider what aspects of a formal procurement process you will use?**

For each significantly sized procured service or product answer the following questions:

1. How will we identify good potential sellers?

2. What type of pricing/service proposal best fits the project (Request for Information (RFI), Request for Proposal (RFP), Request for Bid, (RFB))?

3. What type of contract legal issues could be written into our procurement contract to protect the project and our organization?

4. Are there project risks that can be transferred to the sellers?

5. What will payment arrangements be? Should retainage be considered?

6. How will we ensure that all bidders receive the same project information at the same time, including responses to questions raised by individual bidders?

# 21. Quality Plan

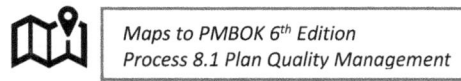

*Maps to PMBOK 6th Edition*
*Process 8.1 Plan Quality Management*

Below is a table of quality parameters to consider for your project as well as your product.

| Parameter | Quality of a PRODUCT | Quality of a SERVICE |
|---|---|---|
| Value | The product is worth the cost to the customer in terms of its usability, reliability, and longevity. | The implementation of the service improves the customer's operation commensurate with the cost. The cost-benefit ratio is appropriate. |
| Usability | The product delivers what is promised. | The service delivers what is promised. |
| Reliability | The product functions when needed without the constant need for maintenance or replacement parts. | The service functions as expected without failure and excessive downtime. |
| Longevity | The product is not made obsolete prematurely and has an appropriate life cycle relative to its cost. | The service is not made obsolete prematurely and has an appropriate life cycle relative to its cost. |

*What quality parameters are key to your project's success?*

## Quality Aids

The following are instructional aids that can help ensure the quality of your project:

| Aids | Description | List aids of this type that you could use for your project. |
|---|---|---|
| Standards | Instructions that detail how a particular aspect of the project must be undertaken. There can be no deviation from "Standards" unless a formal variation process is undertaken, and approval granted. | |
| Guidelines | Unlike "Standards", "Guidelines" are not compulsory. They are intended to guide a project rather than dictate how it must be undertaken. Variations do not require formal approval. | |
| Checklists | "Checklists" are lists that can be used as a prompt when undertaking a particular activity. They tend to be accumulated wisdom from many projects. | |
| Templates | "Templates" are blank documents to be used in particular stages of a project. They will usually contain some examples and instructions. | |
| Procedures | "Procedures" outline the steps that should be undertaken in a particular area of a project such as managing risks or managing time. | |
| User Guides | "User Guides" provide the theory, principles and detailed instructions as to how to apply the procedures to the project. They contain such information as definitions, reasons for undertaking the steps in the procedure, and roles and responsibilities. | |
| Example Documents/Lessons Learned | These are examples from prior projects that are good indicators of the type of information, and level of detail that is required in the completed document. | |

# Quality Terminology Crossword Puzzle

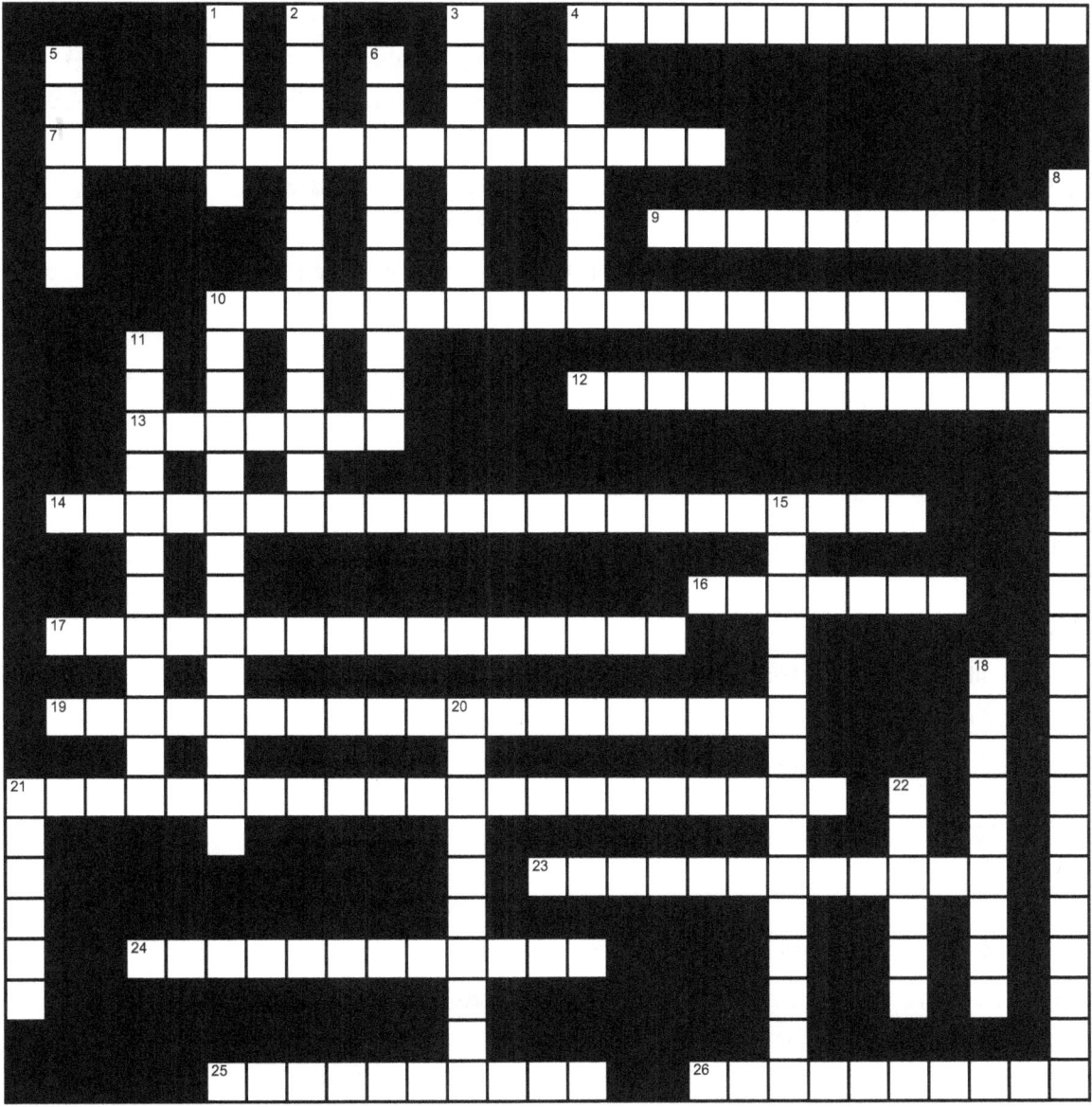

## CLUES

*(The number at the end of the clues are the letter count for the separate words.)*

**Across**

4. A source of variation that is not inherent in the system, is not predictable, and is intermittent (7,6)
7. Unable to be both true (or happening) at the same time (8,9)
9. A quality histogram (6,5)
10. Where a random sample is selected instead of measuring the entire population (11,8)
12. A data display tool to analyze if a process is "in control" or not (7,6)

13 Examples of this include defect density, failure rate, availability, reliability, and test coverage. (7)

14 Plans how quality activities will be streamlined and improved (7,11,4)

16 A certification standard that ensures that companies document what they do and do what they document. (3,4)

17 Concerned with overall process improvement during the execution phase. A focus on steadily improving the activities and processes. (7,9)

19 Helps identify which factors may influence specific variables of a product or process under development or in production. (6,2,11)

21 Ishikawa diagrams and fishbone diagrams (5,3,6,7)

23 A standard by which something can be judged (12)

24 Visual representation of a process (12)

25 Limits your project has set for product acceptance. (10)

26 A manufacturing method that brings inventory down to zero (or near zero) levels. (4-2-4)

**Down**

1 Quality guru widely credited for adding the human dimension to quality management (5)

2 A review process to determine how well the process fulfills requirements (7,6)

3 Displays observed data in a time sequence (3,5)

4 A popular quality philosophy that focuses on controlling processes and reducing defects. (3,5)

5 Quality guru who often said "think of manufacturing as a system" not as bits and pieces. (6)

6 Used to ensure that all steps were performed. (10)

8 The occurrence of one event makes it neither more nor less probable that the other occurs (11,12)

10 Shows the pattern of relationships between two variables (7,7)

11 A source of variation that is inherent in the system and is predictable (6,6)

15 A review of the quality process to ensure that it is working effectively (7,8)

18 A bar chart showing observed frequencies (9)

20 Taking action to reduce the probability of negative consequences (10)

21 Quality guru who often said, "Do it right the first time." (6)

22 A Japanese business philosophy of continuous improvement (6)

See Answer Key: Quality Terminology Crossword Puzzle

# 22. Human Resource Plan

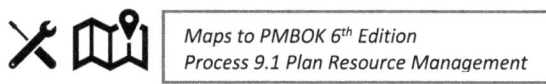

*Maps to PMBOK 6th Edition*
*Process 9.1 Plan Resource Management*

You will need to consider both human and physical resource requirements for your project. Related to human resources, you might use a *Responsibility Assignment Matrix (RAM)* chart to document the project resources and their roles and responsibilities. A popular type of RAM is a RACI chart described below.

## Responsibility Assignment Matrix (RAM) – RACI Format

The person responsible for the execution of an activity needs to know the stakeholders who will need to be consulted, informed, or who will approve the work. The WBS and project management software often do not communicate this information. The RAM, including the RACI format, is one of the best ways to clarify and communicate these responsibilities.

Use the typical chart below to document roles for your project and immediately following the chart you will find guidelines to consider when creating your RAMs.

**Traditional Roles - RACI**
**R** = Responsible for doing the work
**A** = Accountable/Approval
**C** = Consult
**I** = Inform

**Occasional Additions**
**D** = Devil's Advocate
**V** = Veto Power

| Activity | Project Manager | | | Stakeholders | | | | |
|---|---|---|---|---|---|---|---|---|
| Project planning and communication | | | | | | | | |
| | | | | | | | | |
| | | | | | | | | |
| | | | | | | | | |
| | | | | | | | | |

See Appendix A – Sample Templates

**Best Practice: Think A=Approval.**

The A may stand for Approval or Accountable in some organizations. The difference between Responsible and Accountable is often very hard to differentiate. However, the difference between Responsible and Approval seems to be better understood. So, by using Approval instead of Accountable, the roles seem clearer.

Approval responsibilities represent a certain degree of power and putting the A role in a RAM often raises a political question. A good project plan adds clarity and visibility to these issues that otherwise often become sources of conflict.

Another issue that this role delineation raises to the surface is the need for time to be planned into the schedule for the approver to handle the work review or decision logic.

**Best Practice: Have an R for every activity.**

You may have more than one R in a row, but that is not ideal. There are cases where it is accurate, but when you see multiple Rs associated with one activity in your plan you may want to consider breaking the roles down a bit further to aid in role clarity.

**Best Practice: Do not put more than one letter in a cell.**

You would not put an R, C, and I together in one cell. There is a hierarchy.
- R (responsible) trumps C (consult).
- C (consult) trumps I (inform).
- A (accountable/approval) and R (responsible) are quite different roles and ideally, you will assign them to different stakeholders.

**Best Practice: Don't be afraid of empty cells.**

Every person is not involved with every part of every project.

**Best Practice: Push yourself to use more C's and I's to improve your project quality.**

# Escalation Guidelines

Escalation guidelines should be built into written governance processes and communication management plans. Many times, project managers do not make an effective use of escalation guidelines in order to avoid conflict or they may overdo it and escalate when it is not necessary. Escalating an issue at the right time, to the right person with the right amount of information is an important skill for a good project manager. Project managers should escalate timely if something is impeding the project and is beyond the project manager's control. Below are some best practices related to proper escalation.

1. Establish a process for escalation at the start of the project (Kickoff meeting)
2. Define/identify the chain of command/decisions makers
3. Establish mutually agreed upon monitoring and control procedures
4. Define/explain the key items that would require escalation
    - The possibility of Missing a milestone
    - Safety issues
    - Accidents/injuries
    - Loss of personnel
    - A significant change in requirements
    - Significant task or schedule delays
    - Critical path issues
    - Disasters – A notification process should be in place
    - Classify project jeopardy situations – Critical or red, Serious or yellow
5. Gather information about the issue
    - Who is involved?
    - What has occurred?
    - What are the ramifications if not resolved?
    - When is action required?
    - Impact on other projects, operations, company image
    - Who is responsible to resolve the issue?
    - Recommended actions
    - Required response date/time
6. Identify who should receive the project escalation and others who should be informed. Keep the distribution to a minimum. No need to include people who are not directly related or who don't have a need to be involved.
7. Escalations are not personal. It is part of the business environment.
8. Escalation is partly a judgment call. In some cases, there is a specific protocol to follow. How serious is the issue? What are the alternatives? Is escalation beneficial?
9. Inform the other parties before the escalation is implemented. Professional courtesy will prevent reverse escalation and unnecessary conflict.
10. Follow up. Make sure that the issue receives the appropriate attention.
11. Document the final solutions/decisions and the outcome.
12. When appropriate, issue a thank-you. Cooperation, support, willingness to find a solution are all worthy of a thank you.

*Prepared by: Frank P. Saladis PMP. Reprinted with permission.*

# Workload Histogram for Human Resources

*1* **The graph above is an example of a resource histogram from MS Project.**

During resource planning, you may need to enlist workload leveling to assist you with balancing out the times when human and equipment resources are over-allocated, and to accommodate other commitments, holidays, and other schedule interferences.

To create resource histograms, the project manager must plan not only the duration of the work but how much work will get done in each planned work unit (usually in weeks). If you maintain the initial assumed estimated resources, workload leveling always has the effect of lengthening the project schedule. However, histograms can also help in determining times when additional resources could be most helpful.

If you want to try to use resource histograms, you can sign up for a trial account with Microsoft Project, or if you have access to MS Project or Primavera, you can try these or similar products to explore these tools and techniques.

# 23. Risk Plan

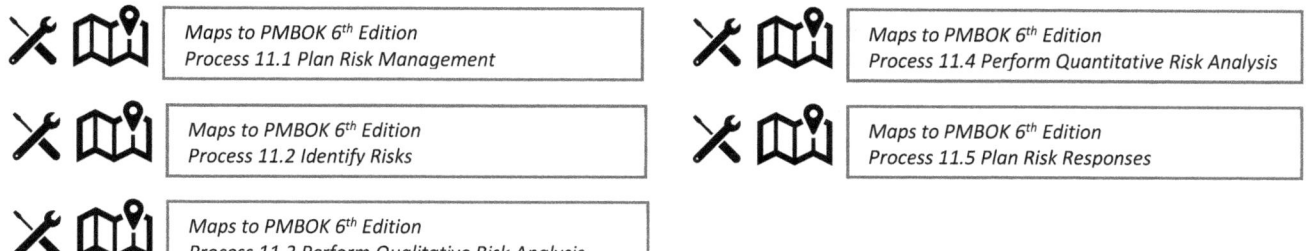

*Maps to PMBOK 6th Edition Process 11.1 Plan Risk Management*

*Maps to PMBOK 6th Edition Process 11.2 Identify Risks*

*Maps to PMBOK 6th Edition Process 11.3 Perform Qualitative Risk Analysis*

*Maps to PMBOK 6th Edition Process 11.4 Perform Quantitative Risk Analysis*

*Maps to PMBOK 6th Edition Process 11.5 Plan Risk Responses*

Risk planning is an important part of project management. We identify risks and plan our responses in order to optimize the chances for project success.

There are many tools and techniques used to identify, prioritize and monitor risks. You may use quantifiable techniques such as *decision trees* that help you arrive at a monetary value to assign to each of your risks. Or you may use a qualitative tool, such as the *Probability/Impact matrix* below.

*Consider risks that could impact your project, use the Risk Register / Log below to list a few of these. Your list will include an evaluation of each risk's probability and impact.*

# Risk Register/Log

| Project Name: | | | | | | | | |
|---|---|---|---|---|---|---|---|---|
| Project Manager Name: | | | | | | | | |
| ID | Current Status | Risk Probability/ Impact | Risk Description | Project Impact | Risk Area | Risk Response Strategy | Response Strategy | Contingency Plan |
| | Open | LOW/MED | **EXAMPLE:** Current project skill set may not be adequate to complete all project work. | **EXAMPLE:** If required skills are not identified or obtained, the project schedule may slip and possibly restrict the accomplishment of project goals. | Project Resources Budget Schedule | Mitigation | **EXAMPLE:** Find an internal resource that meets the required skill set or train existing resources. | **EXAMPLE:** Find a resource that meets required skill set through external hiring sources. |
| | | | | | | | | |
| | | | | | | | | |
| | | | | | | | | |

See Appendix A – Sample Templates

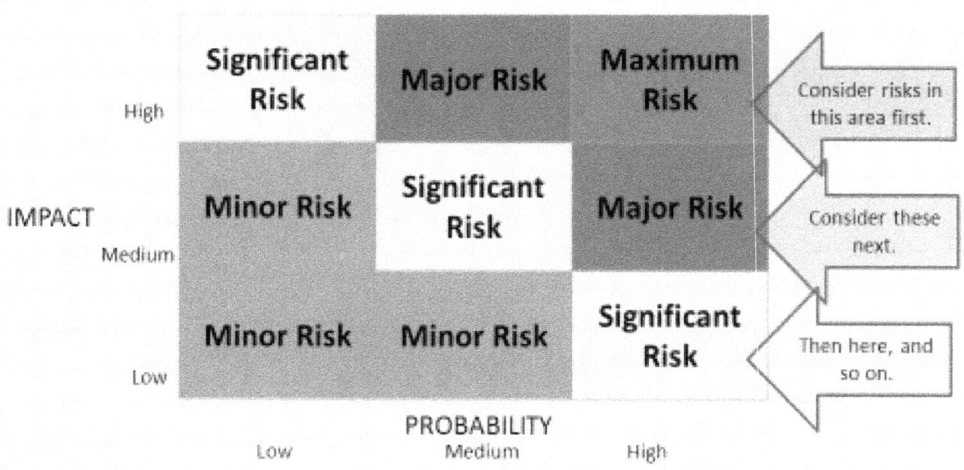

*If you want to more fully document each risk, then use the Risk Control Form below. For practice, use the forms below to expand on one of the risks you identified.*

# Risk Control Forms

| Risk ID: | Date Raised:<br><br>Last Reviewed: | Raised By: | Owner: |
|---|---|---|---|

| Short Description: |
|---|
|  |

| Status: (select one)<br>• Draft<br>• Open<br>• Rejected<br>• Closed | Triggers<br>*(early indicators that the risk event may be starting to occur)* |
|---|---|

**Which Option or Combination of Options is Best?**

| Negative Risks | Positive Risks<br>*(aka Opportunities)* |
|---|---|
| **Mitigate**: Take actions to minimize the impact and reduce the likelihood. | **Exploit**: Take action to definitely make the occurrence happen. |
| **Transfer**: Have another organization take responsibility for the risk. | **Share**: Spread the business/profits/money/pleasure around. |
| **Avoid**: Take the risk component out of the project. | **Enhance**: Take action to increase the probability and positive impact. |
| **Accept**: | **Accept**: |
| **Escalate**: | **Escalate**: |

Describe how this strategy will be implemented:

What secondary risks may come out of this strategy?

| Probability (score 1-10) | Very Likely: 10 | Impact (score 1-10) | High: 10 |
|---|---|---|---|
|  | Probable: 8 |  | Medium: 5 |
|  | Possible: 3 |  | Low: 1 |
|  | Unlikely: 1 |  |  |
|  | **Risk Score** (Probability x Impact): | | |
| Closed Date: | Outcome: | | |

*Every battle plan changes after the shooting starts.*

# 24. Change Control Plan

Change is an inevitable part of a project. You need to have a plan in place to handle these changes. From decisions related to which changes to approve, to managing the changes through execution and delivery. You will need to develop a change approval template like the one below.

## Change Request Form

Control Number:        Date Created:        Originator:

Name of Project:

Change Proposal Title:

Proposed Change Description and References:

Justification:

___

Impact of Not Implementing Proposed Change:
___
Alternatives:
___

*Initial Review Results*

Review Date: _____ Assigned to: _____

---

Decision:

☐ Approve for Implementation    ☐ Reject    ☐ Defer Until: _____

Reason:


Cost/Schedule Impact Analysis Required?  ☐ No    ☐ Yes

---

Impact on Cost:

Impact on Schedule:

Impact on Resources:

Reviewing Body:
Name: _____ Signature: _____ Date: _____

See Appendix A - Templates

# 25. Communications Plan

 *Maps to PMBOK 6th Edition*
*Process 10.1 Plan Communications Management*

 *Maps to PMBOK 6th Edition*
*Process 13.2 Plan Stakeholder Engagement*

90% of a project manager's job is spent on communications. Therefore, it is important to take the time to create your communications management plan for your project. The communications planning process concerns defining the types of information you will deliver, who will receive it, and the format and timing for the communications.

It is important to make sure everybody gets the right message at the right time. Consider including the following components with your communications plan:

- ☐ Collection and filing structure for gathering and storing project information
- ☐ Example of a project status report (showing the format and type of information to be included)
- ☐ Escalation procedures
- ☐ Stakeholder communications analysis
- ☐ Glossary of new project terms

Use the communications plan template below to create your project's communications plan.

| Audience | Vehicle of Communication | Frequency | Other Information |
|---|---|---|---|
| *(Example) Project steering committee* | *Formal presentations by the PM* | *Project plan presentation, major change requests, major milestones, and at formal acceptance.* | *The steering committee meets on the 2nd Tuesday of each month.* |
| *Core Project Team Members* | | | |
| | | | |
| | | | |
| | | | |
| **Comments:** | | | |

See Appendix A - Templates

## Stakeholder Engagement Level Gaps

Your next step will be to ensure that you consult with interested project stakeholders. Many times, individuals who feel that they should have been consulted on the decision to undertake the project, or whose point of view was not heeded, will not support the project, or will continue to actively oppose it.

In the *stakeholder engagement assessment matrix* below list the stakeholders in the "Manage Closely" quadrant that you created in Step 5 – Identify Stakeholders. Assess each stakeholder's current (C) and desired (D) levels of engagement. Then, for instances where there is a gap, consider the stakeholder communication work that should be done early in the project phases.

| Stakeholder | Unaware | Resistant | Neutral | Supportive | Leading |
|---|---|---|---|---|---|
| Stakeholder A | | | C | | D |
| | | | | | |
| | | | | | |
| | | | | | |
| | | | | | |
| | | | | | |
| | | | | | |
| | | | | | |
| | | | | | |
| | | | | | |
| | | | | | |
| | | | | | |
| | | | | | |

> Managing large-scale political projects takes a different skill set and management style. Advanced project management has to focus on developing leadership, matrix management, and other business-oriented skills.

# 26. Baseline Project Plan

At this point, you have done extensive planning and a baseline project plan is established. The baseline is the approved version of all of the elements planned for the project including the WBS, schedule, time-based budget, and plan for how the resources, quality risk, communications, and procurement is expected to go.

This baseline remains the same and will become the base for the Earned Value Performance Reporting which will be discussed later. Below is an example project baseline.

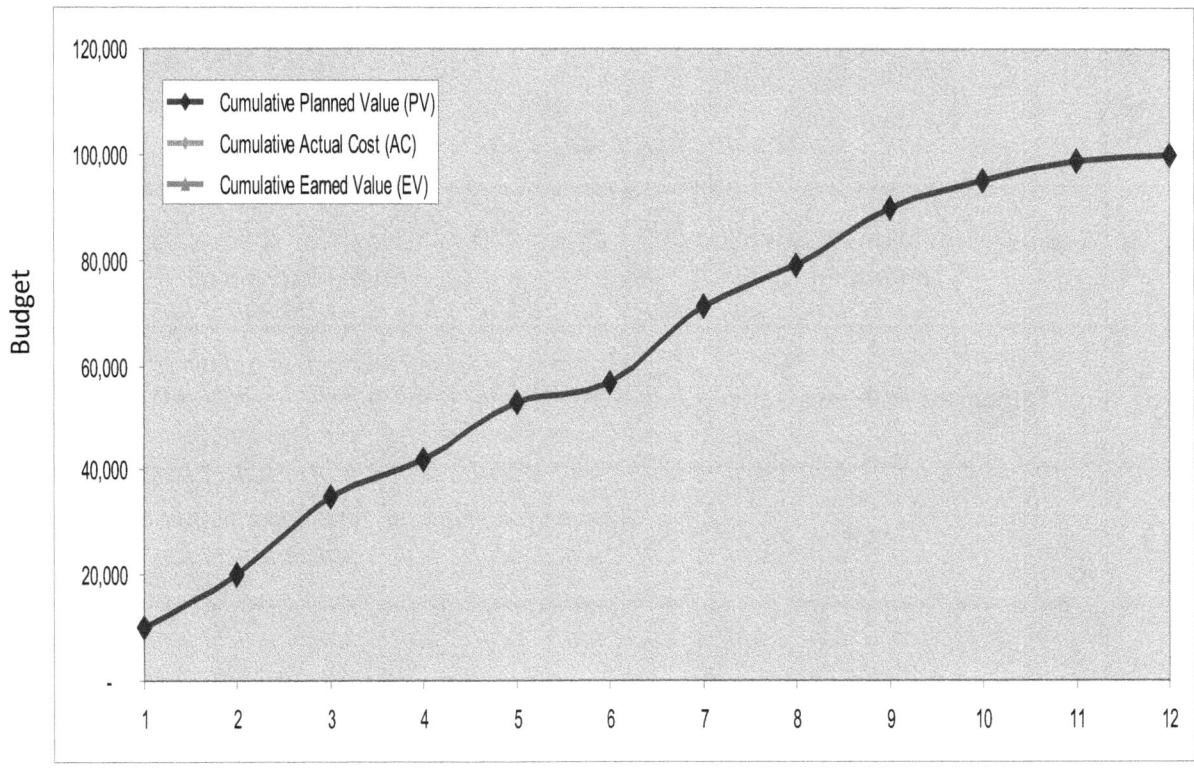

# 27. Project Plan Approval

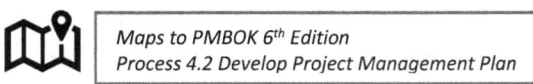

*Maps to PMBOK 6th Edition*
*Process 4.2 Develop Project Management Plan*

Are your project team and project sponsor on board with the final project plan? Use this chart at your next meeting to gauge their level of agreement and buy-in.

## Gradients of Agreement Chart

|     | Level of Agreement | Commonly Verbalized as... |
|-----|---|---|
| **+3** | Endorsement | I like it. I support it. |
| **+2** | Endorsement with a minor point of contention | Basically, I like it. However, there is one small part I'm unsure of or don't like. |
| **+1** | Agreement with reservations | It is not my ideal and there are parts I'm fairly negative about. I will continue to lobby to remove the gap between this idea and my reservations about it while I support the idea moving forward. |
| **0** | Abstain | I have no opinion, or I feel other people should make this decision. |
| **-1** | Stand aside | I don't like this, but I don't want to hold up the group. |
| **-2** | Formal disagreement but willing to go with the majority | I want my disagreement noted in writing, but I will support the decision. |
| **-3** | Formal disagreement, with a request to be absolved of responsibility | I don't want to stop anyone else, but I don't want to be personally involved in implementing it. |
| **-4** | Block | I veto this proposal. I want to stop this from proceeding. |

Adapted from Sam Kaner, 1996

## Request Sponsor Sign-Off

When you have the plan completed entirely, review the baseline project plan with the major sponsor. Make sure you include a sample of the format planned for the project status reports, what the change thresholds will be and then request sponsor sign-off.

**Change thresholds:**

1. The project needs to be stopped, pending authorization to proceed, when the schedule variance is more than _____% off plan.

2. The project needs to be stopped, pending authorization to proceed, when the cost variance is more than _____% off plan.

_____
Sponsor Approval Signature                                           Date

# EXECUTING

Now is where your planning pays off. You are ready to begin performing project activities.

## 28 Acquire Project Resources

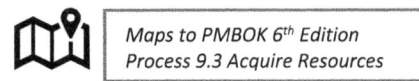
Maps to PMBOK 6th Edition
Process 9.3 Acquire Resources

When considering resources for your project, consider in this conversation:
- ☐ If you are working with functional managers, stress the following:
    - o Which tasks need experts, and which may be suitable for less skilled staff.
    - o The importance of creating experts within the team by putting the same people on related tasks.
- ☐ Ensure that each core project team member has a chance to address any serious project concerns.
- ☐ Either involve the core team members in the creation of the WBS or get their approval on the WBS if they are added to the project later.

### Emotional Intelligence

Emotional intelligence is the capacity to be aware of, control, and express emotions. It also involves being able to handle interpersonal relationships with empathy. It is often viewed, as important if not more important, than technical skills when hiring. Being aware of this will help you select, develop and manage your team.

Are you able to identify emotionally intelligent behaviors? Use this checklist to think through these attributes for each of your team members and for yourself.

### Are They Emotionally Intelligent?

- ☐ <u>Self-Awareness</u> – Do they have a solid understanding of their own emotions, their strengths, weaknesses, and what drives them?

- ☐ <u>Ability to Regulate Emotions</u> – Are they able to manage their emotions so that emotions do not control their words and actions?

- ☐ <u>Motivation</u> – Are they willing to defer immediate results for long-term success? Are they highly productive and love challenges?

- ☐ <u>Empathy</u> – Do they have an awareness of the feelings of others and consider those feelings in their words and actions?

- ☐ <u>Social Skills</u> – Are they able to relate and find common ground with a wide range of people?

Everyone has both strengths and areas to improve when it comes to emotional intelligence.

Focus first on you and your team's strengths. Doing so will generate positive emotions and this will give you the strength to deal with problem areas.

If you want to learn more about Emotional Intelligence or EQ and take an EQ test, the book *Emotional Intelligence 2.0* referenced in our reading list is a great resource.

# 29. Develop Project Team

 *Maps to PMBOK 6th Edition Process 9.4 Develop Team*

 *Maps to PMBOK 6th Edition Process 9.5 Manage Team*

The development of the project team often involves taking steps to improve the team's interactions and skill competencies for the project.

1. Has the entire team been briefed on the project rules?
2. Will the team benefit from having the project manager create a project glossary?
3. What skills or training may be needed prior to the project work beginning?
4. What team members need to get to know each other in order to facilitate effective work and communications?
5. What is in it for the team member? Possibly the ability to learn new skills, add something wonderful to their portfolio, or help their career?

Your project team will look to you for project leadership. As a leader, you have to make tough decisions and at times have difficult conversations. Explore behaviors displayed by leaders, do you exhibit these as you interact with your team on a day-to-day basis?

- <u>Positive connections with others</u> - If you are in a bad mood, it will be contagious. On the other hand, if you are positive and optimistic, these emotions will be infectious to your team as well.
- <u>Display integrity</u> – Can your team members count on you to live up to your promises?
- <u>Cooperate with others</u> - Instilling a cooperative approach goes much further than instilling a competitive atmosphere within your team.
- <u>Be a coach and mentor to your team</u> - Is someone struggling with a task or with another team member. How can you use your experiences to help them?
- <u>Be an inspiration</u> - Take time to roll up your sleeves and help the team overcome obstacles and meet critical deadlines.
- <u>Be future focused</u> - Share the end goal with the team often. When your team does not clearly understand where they are headed and how they will get there, it makes them frustrated and dissatisfied.
- <u>Ask for feedback</u> – Inquire on how you are doing and be willing to be open to making changes.

# 30. Complete Work Packages

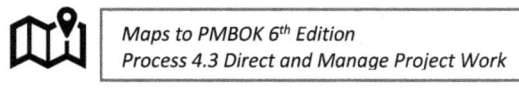

Maps to PMBOK 6th Edition
Process 4.3 Direct and Manage Project Work

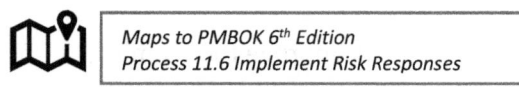

Maps to PMBOK 6th Edition
Process 11.6 Implement Risk Responses

This is where the work gets done. This is the effort of creating the project deliverables as scoped in the project work breakdown structure. As you complete work, be sure to keep an eye on your risk register (Step 23) so that you can anticipate risks and respond as planned if they occur.

Remember that completion measures accomplishment, not effort expended. Consider using the 0-50-100 rule for tracking the completion of work packages.

- 0% complete = The task has not yet begun.
- 50% complete = The task has been started but not finished.
- 100% complete = The task is complete.

Track percent-complete either in a Gantt chart or in the WBS on a regular basis as the project work is completed.

# 31. Scope Verification

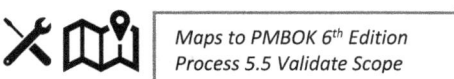 *Maps to PMBOK 6th Edition Process 5.5 Validate Scope*

This is the work of obtaining formal acceptance of the completed project deliverables. What form of inspection is appropriate? Below is a sample Deliverable Acceptance Form.

| **Deliverable Acceptance Form** |
|---|
| Project Title:<br>Date:<br><br>Project Sponsor:<br>Project Manager: |
| **Description of Deliverable**<br><br><br><br><br>**Deliverable Acceptance Criteria**<br><br><br><br> |
| **Deliverable Acceptance** |
| Approved/Rejected:<br>Comments<br><br><br>Deliverable Accepted By:                                              Date: |
| Approved/Rejected:<br>Comments<br><br><br>Sponsor Acceptance                                                   Date: |

See Appendix A - Templates

# 32. Information Distribution

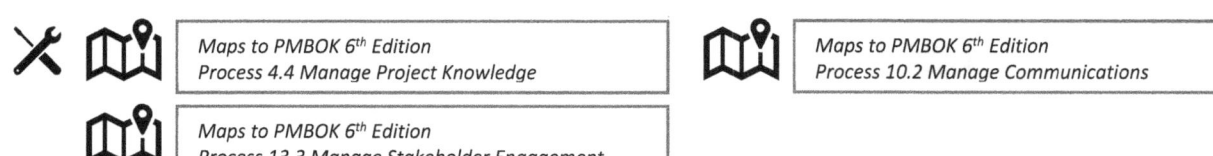

*Maps to PMBOK 6th Edition*
*Process 4.4 Manage Project Knowledge*

*Maps to PMBOK 6th Edition*
*Process 10.2 Manage Communications*

*Maps to PMBOK 6th Edition*
*Process 13.3 Manage Stakeholder Engagement*

This includes providing team members work information such as the WBS Dictionary (below), executing the communication management plan (Step 25), providing project status reports (Step 37) and facilitating project meetings, as well as responding to unexpected requests for information.

The WBS Dictionary helps to prevent scope creep by clarifying the scope for the project team which helps prevent unnecessary or out of scope work.

## WBS Dictionary Example

| WBS Dictionary (Task Description) | | | |
|---|---|---|---|
| Project Name | Job and Task No | Date Issued | Person Assigned |
| Length | Due Date | Budget | Sign Off/Approver |
| Task Description | | | |
| Goals and objectives | | | |
| Product description | | | |
| Acceptance criteria | | | |
| Interdependencies: Before this task _____ After this task _____ | | | |
| Contact for any questions or concerns: | | | |

See Appendix A - Templates

> Studies show that formally written work instructions are better followed than casual instructions.

# Meetings

*Meetings* are an important mechanism to distribute information. Holding a successful meeting is attainable with these tips in mind. Make your meetings GREAT.

**G – Goals** for the meeting should be **SMART**: Specific, Measurable, Actionable, Realistic and Time-Bound.

**R – Roles and Rules:** If possible, roles should be rotated among project team members so that everyone gets an opportunity to show leadership. Make sure to invite someone who is a decision maker. Ground-rules for discussion should be agreed upon beforehand so the items discussed get accomplished.

**E – Expectations** should be clearly set: Your discussions should remain focused on new issues rather than an endless string of updates.

**A – Agendas** should be distributed in advance: Include the purpose of the meeting at the top, a good agenda will help keep your meeting on point.

**T – Time** is money so be sensitive to the team member's scheduling needs: Keep it brief; begin and end meetings on time. Don't hold the weekly staff meeting just because it's Monday at 9:00 AM. Cancel the meeting if you can't think of an actual problem to solve or decision that needs to be made.

*Sources: How to Hold a Great Meeting, Tara Weiss*

Please see the next page for a sample format for your meeting agenda.

# Meeting Agenda

### MEETING INFORMATION

| | | | |
|---|---|---|---|
| Purpose: | [Enter the objective of the meeting here.] | | |
| Date: | 01/01/2000 | Location: | [Enter Room Number] |
| Time: | 6:00 AM | Meeting Type: | [Identify type of meeting] |
| Call-In Number: | [List call in number] | Call-In Code: | [Enter call in code] |
| Called by: | | | |
| Attendees: | [List Names] | | |

### PREPARATION FOR MEETING

Please Read/Bring:

| ACTION ITEMS FROM PREVIOUS MEETING | RESPONSIBLE | DUE DATE |
|---|---|---|
| 1  [List Action Item 1] | [Name] | [Date] |
| 2 | | |

| AGENDA ITEMS | PRESENTER | TIME ALLOTTED |
|---|---|---|
| 1  [List Agenda Item 1] | [Name] | [x minutes] |
| 2 | | |

| NEW ACTION ITEMS | RESPONSIBLE | DUE DATE |
|---|---|---|
| 1  [List New Action Item 1] | [Name] | [Date] |
| 2 | | |

### OTHER NOTES OR INFORMATION

See Appendix A - Templates

# 33. Quality Assurance – Managing Quality

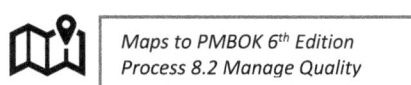

*Maps to PMBOK 6th Edition*
*Process 8.2 Manage Quality*

This involves the work of applying the quality plan, or more specifically ensuring that the project has the necessary quality tools and techniques to perform quality audits and analyze the processes. The result of managing quality includes making improvements to the project deliverables, processes, and/or plan.

Many students have difficulty differentiating between manage quality, also known as, quality assurance and quality control. This chart provides a contrasting analysis:

|  | **Manage Quality (QA)** | **Quality Control (QC)** |
|---|---|---|
| **Definition** | QA is a set of activities for ensuring quality in the processes by which products are developed. | QC is a set of activities for ensuring quality in products. The activities focus on identifying defects in the actual products produced. |
| **Focus on** | QA aims to prevent defects with a focus on the process used to make the product. It is a proactive quality process. | QC aims to identify (and correct) defects in the finished product. Quality control, therefore, is a reactive process. |
| **Goal** | The goal of QA is to improve development and test processes so that defects do not arise when the product is being developed. | The goal of QC is to identify defects after a product is developed and before it's released. |
| **How** | Establish a good quality management system and the assessment of its adequacy. Periodic conformance audits of the operations of the system. | Finding & eliminating sources of quality problems through tools & equipment so that customer's requirements are continually met. |
| **What** | Prevention of quality problems through planned and systematic activities including documentation. | The activities or techniques used to achieve and maintain the product quality, process and service. |
| **Responsibility** | Everyone on the team involved in developing the product is responsible for quality assurance. | Quality control is usually the responsibility of a specific team that tests the product for defects. |
| **Example** | Verification is an example of QA. | Validation/Software Testing is an example of QC. |
| **As a tool** | QA is a managerial tool. | QC is a corrective tool. |

# 34. Procurement Solicitation and Selection

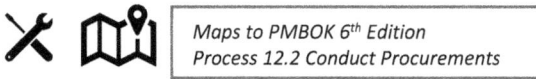

Maps to PMBOK 6th Edition
Process 12.2 Conduct Procurements

At this time, you will be reviewing solicitation responses, evaluating and making vendor selections. A *Weighted Decision Matrix* is a helpful tool for this activity.

## Example of a Weighted Decision Matrix

| Criteria | Weight | Vendor 1 | Vendor 2 | Vendor 3 | Vendor 4 |
|---|---|---|---|---|---|
| A | 25% | 90 | 90 | 50 | 20 |
| B | 15% | 70 | 90 | 50 | 20 |
| C | 15% | 50 | 90 | 50 | 20 |
| D | 10% | 25 | 90 | 50 | 70 |
| E | 5% | 20 | 20 | 50 | 90 |
| F | 20% | 50 | 70 | 50 | 50 |
| G | 10% | 20 | 50 | 50 | 90 |
| **Weighted Project Scores** | **100%** | **56** | **78.5** | **50** | **41.5** |

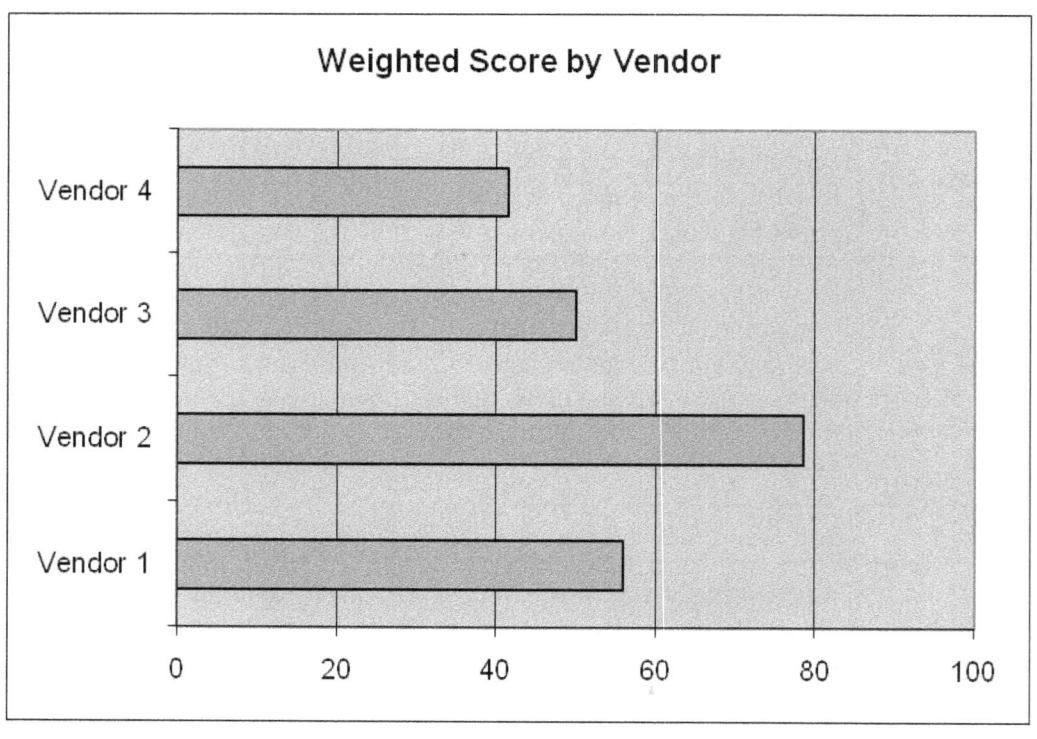

# CONTROL & MONITORING

At the same time that you are executing project work, you are constantly monitoring performance and taking action to control any variance from your plan. These activities are very tightly integrated and occur simultaneously not linearly.

## 35. Overall Change Control

Keep a *change log* of the change decisions (tracked from step 24).

*Maps to PMBOK 6th Edition*
*Process 4.6 Perform Integrated Change Control*

| Change ID | Description | Date Changed | Effect to Quality, Schedule, and/or Cost | Notes |
|---|---|---|---|---|
| | | | | |
| | | | | |
| | | | | |
| | | | | |
| | | | | |
| | | | | |
| | | | | |
| | | | | |
| | | | | |
| | | | | |
| | | | | |
| | | | | |
| | | | | |
| | | | | |
| | | | | |
| | | | | |

# 36. Scope Control

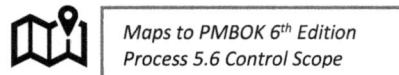
*Maps to PMBOK 6th Edition
Process 5.6 Control Scope*

The project manager works to influence factors that create project scope changes and the impact of those changes. This includes noticing when changes are occurring, filtering out changes from inappropriate people, and ensuring that changes that are accepted into the project are beneficial.

Use a Change Request Form (Step 24) to document changes during this process.

# 37. Performance Reporting

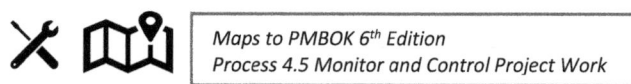
*Maps to PMBOK 6th Edition
Process 4.5 Monitor and Control Project Work*

This involves collecting and distributing performance information on project status (often including schedule, budget, quality, risk, and team performance information). This also includes using the status information to forecast future results.

## Status Reporting

*Status reporting* on a regular basis provides necessary information sharing and performance reporting. Did you clear a backlog of customer orders? Did you come up with a new idea to solve a tricky problem? Did you write a first draft of an article that is due next week? As you progress through work activities on your project, it's not enough to observe what is going on, you need to communicate and document — often.

On the next page is a sample status report you can use for your project.

# PROJECT STATUS REPORT: [PROJECT NAME]

**Project Manager:** [Name]  **Week Ending:** [MM-DD-YY]

**Project Status++**  *Red =Schedule/Cost variance >25% and/or Critical Issue. Yellow = Schedule/Cost variance > 15% and < 25% and/or medium issue. Green = Schedule/Cost variance <15% and/or low risk issues. Blue = Complete. Purple = On hold or deferred. Black = Cancelled or Aborted*

++Project Status definition and thresholds should reflect your organization's policies and standards

### 1.1.1 Project Overview

### 1.1.2 Brief Summary of Current Status
*Accomplishments, Project Details, Relevant Information that falls outside of noted categories.*

### 1.1.3 Project Milestones
Note: The below schedule is a snap-shot from the project schedule (either Microsoft Project Plan or another related schedule document). The MS Project Plan (MPP) or other related schedule documents, is the plan of record for the project schedule.

| % Complete | Description | Start Date | Planned Finish Date | % Schedule Variance ^ | % Cost Variance^^ |
|---|---|---|---|---|---|
| | Project Phase: Initiation | | | | |
| | Project Phase: Planning | | | | |
| | Project Phase: Execution | | | | |
| | Project Phase: Closure | | | | |

^ Deviation from the baseline schedule.
^^ Deviation from the baseline costs.

### 1.1.4 Key Deliverables & Project Tasks

| % Complete | Description | Start Date | Planned Finish Date | % Schedule Variance | % Cost Variance |
|---|---|---|---|---|---|
| | | | | | |
| | | | | | |

### 1.1.5 Explanation of Significant Changes
*Describe any significant changes including Project Change Requests, significant date changes, or significant variances.*

## Current Critical Issue(s) Being Worked
*Information needed for EACH critical issue.*

| Issue (Description) | Owner | Action | Status (Green, Yellow, Red) |
|---|---|---|---|
| | | | |
| | | | |

See Appendix A - Templates

# 38. Schedule Control

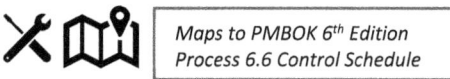

*Maps to PMBOK 6th Edition*
*Process 6.6 Control Schedule*

Determine the current schedule status and what the variance is from the plan. You will probably use a Gantt chart to help with this. Look at where you have variances and work on influencing the factors that might affect the schedule, determining what may be causing any large schedule changes, and managing the schedule changes as they do occur.

Look at this schedule as compared to its baseline. If today is August 6th, what observations do you have related to schedule status from this chart?

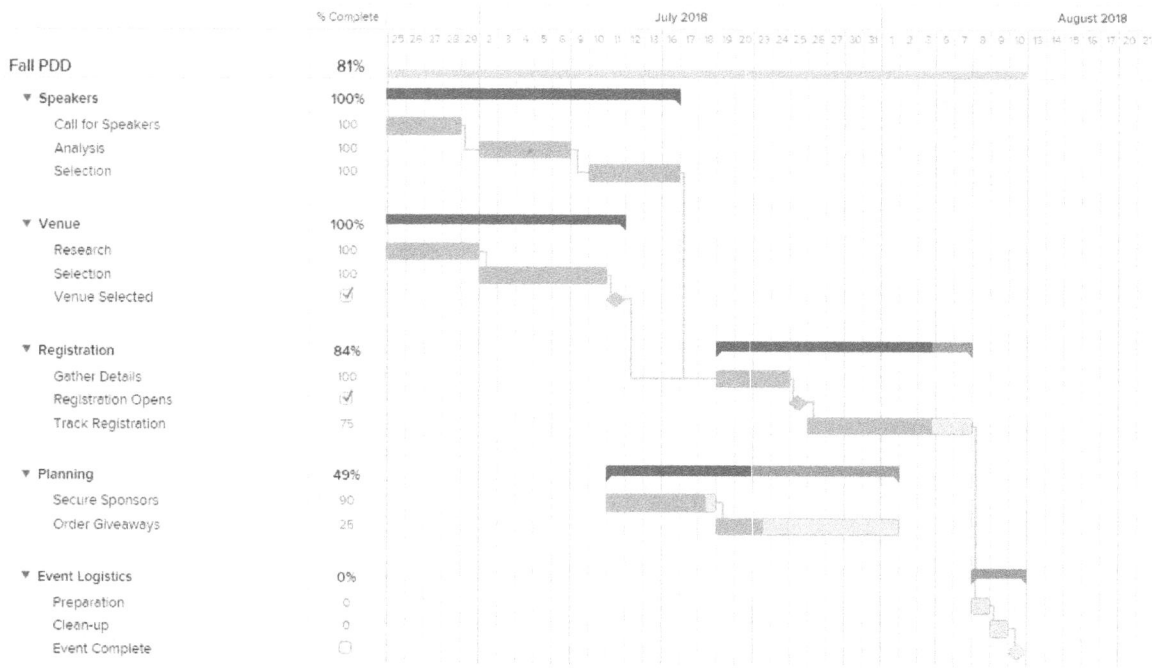

See Answer Key: Schedule Control

# 39. Contract Administration

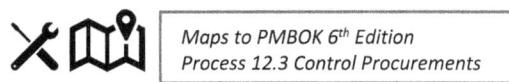

*Maps to PMBOK 6th Edition*
*Process 12.3 Control Procurements*

Contract administration involves managing agreements and vendor performance. This also involves managing contract-related changes. To assist in the management of agreements you should utilize or develop a contract performance monitoring process for your project.

**Make Sure you Maintain Formal Procurement Records**
The formal procurement record is a set of files containing critical documents and information pertinent to the procurement contract. It is from this procurement record that you can find information such as product technical specifications, delivery quantities, and schedules.

Each contract should have its own procurement record files. This allows for easier access to:
- information critical to the contract.
- Includes all pertinent documents and information.
- The purchase contract is a legal document identifying the contractual rights and obligations of each party to the contract. The contract and procurement record files should be kept for the period of time required by national regulations and organizational requirements.

**Formal Procurement Record Systems Serve Three Useful Purposes:**
- The procurement record provides essential supporting evidence if it becomes necessary to take legal action against the supplier.
- The procurement record helps to provide a full audit trail.
- The information contained in the procurement record can be used to help evaluate a supplier's performance and if additional opportunities to conduct business with the supplier should be considered.

## Develop Key Performance Indicators

*Key performance indicators* are used to track and evaluate the supplier's performance in complying with the contract requirements. For performance indicators to be effective, they need to be SMART (Specific, Measurable, Attainable, Relevant, Time-bound). A range of performance indicators can be developed to monitor a supplier's performance, and the exact indicators used will vary according to the commodity provided, the level of risk associated with contract failure by the supplier, and the value of the procurement. The specific information needed to develop performance indicators is drawn from the procurement record files. Performance indicators should be developed that track compliance with the following types of categories:

- Technical specifications.
- Timeliness of deliveries.
- Labeling and packaging requirements.
- Shelf-life requirements.
- Contract terms and conditions.

## Sample Performance Monitoring Checklist

| Monitoring Indicator | # Compliant | # Noncompliant | Percent Compliant | Information/Comments |
|---|---|---|---|---|
| **Supplier Deliveries** | | | | |
| Shipments delivered on time in compliance with contract delivery requirements. | | | | |
| Correct quantity delivered per the contract. | | | | |
| | | | | |
| **Technical Specifications** | | | | |
| Supplier provided advance copies of documents according to contract terms. | | | | |
| Shipments arrived with all required documents correctly and completely filled out and signed. | | | | |
| **Contract Financial Terms** | | | | |
| Invoices that comply with contract pricing terms. | | | | |

See Appendix A - Templates

# 40. Manage Project Team

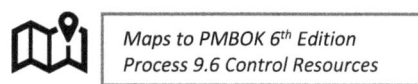
*Maps to PMBOK 6th Edition*
*Process 9.6 Control Resources*

Managing the project team involves tracking team member performance, providing feedback, resolving issues, and coordinating changes to enhance project performance. It usually involves communicating both formally and informally with team members.

## Accountability Questions

1. Do you often experience gaps between team member project schedule commitments and actual performance?

2. Is the culture of the organization one where training people that slipped project schedules is acceptable?

3. Are the team members personally involved with the planning, and are they individually committed to the schedule?

4. Are the team member's functional managers informed of the schedule, and supportive of the project schedule?

5. What are the common barriers causing the team members to miss their schedule commitments on your projects?

6. Who is the best person in the organization to help remove these barriers?

## Fixing Performance Problems

Executive coach Bud Bilanich states that there are eleven reasons why employees don't do what they're supposed to do, that must be explored before disciplinary action is considered.

They are:

1. People don't know *what* they're supposed to do.
2. People don't know *why* they should do what they are supposed to do.
3. People don't know *how* to do what they're supposed to do.
4. People think the prescribed methods will not (or do not) work, or they believe that their way is better.
5. People think other things are more important.
6. People think they are performing in an acceptable manner.
7. Nonperformance is rewarded.
8. Good performance feels like punishment.
9. There are no positive consequences for good performance.
10. There are no negative consequences for poor performance.
11. There are obstacles to performing that the individual cannot control.

If you are interested in learning more about these problems, why they happen, and what to do about them. You may want to pick up his book *Solving Performance Problems – A Leaders Toolkit,* ISBN 1885228767 (sold on amazon.com Solving Performance Problems - A Leaders Toolkit)

# 41. Manage by Exception to the Project Plan

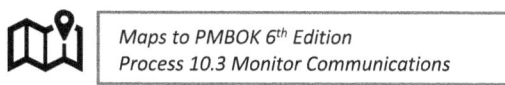
*Maps to PMBOK 6th Edition*
*Process 10.3 Monitor Communications*

If the project has been well-planned and work is proceeding on track, communications may expect to be focused on those aspects of the project that are not exactly as planned. When questions arise, the project plan should answer the most predictable questions. This frees the project manager to address the things that are differing from the baseline project plan – usually meaning they are spending most of their time managing the project changes to improve the project results.

# 42. Quality Control

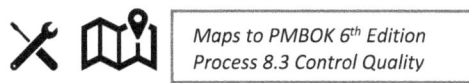
*Maps to PMBOK 6th Edition*
*Process 8.3 Control Quality*

During this time, you are ensuring the project outputs are complete, correct and meet customer expectations. Consider the following questions for your project.

1. Do the deliverables meet the requirements of your key stakeholders?

2. What deliverables need to go through a quality check?

3. What is the most appropriate way to check the quality?

4. When should it be carried out?

5. Who should be involved?

**Practice This**

You are creating a new toy product. You use a check sheet to collect information related to quality. Two production runs have been completed with the results below.

| Defects/Date | Date Run 1 (9/1) | Date Run 2 (10/1) | Total |
|---|---|---|---|
| Small Scratches | 1 | 5 | 6 |
| Wrong Color | 2 | 3 | 5 |
| Missing Components | 0 | 0 | 0 |
| Labeling Error | 5 | 1 | 6 |

What observations concerning quality do you have related to this data?

What might you try before the next run to improve quality?

See Answer Key: **Quality Control**

# 43. Risk Monitoring and Control

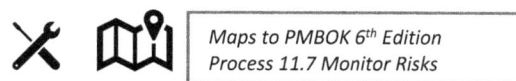

*Maps to PMBOK 6th Edition
Process 11.7 Monitor Risks*

When monitoring for risks, use this checklist for a few reminders.

- ☐ Known risks are monitored and, where possible, mitigation strategies are followed to reduce the probability or impact.
- ☐ Update the risk register (located with step 23). Are there any new risks?
- ☐ Monitor the associated contingencies for both known risks (in your register) and also for the pool of yet unknown risks.
- ☐ There is a plan in place to continue to monitor and control risks.
- ☐ All risks are assigned to someone.
- ☐ Move those things that are occurring to your Issue Log (below).

Once a risk occurs it becomes an issue. Use the issue log below to record risks that have turned into issues.

## Issue Log

| Issue # | Issue Description | Impact on Project | Date Reported | Reported By | Assigned To | Priority (M/H/L) | Due Date | Status |
|---|---|---|---|---|---|---|---|---|
| 1 | Include Risk ID | | | | | | | |
| 2 | | | | | | | | |
| 3 | | | | | | | | |
| 4 | | | | | | | | |
| 5 | | | | | | | | |
| 6 | | | | | | | | |
| 7 | | | | | | | | |
| 8 | | | | | | | | |

See Appendix A - Templates

# 44. Cost Monitoring & Control

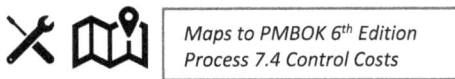

*Maps to PMBOK 6th Edition*
*Process 7.4 Control Costs*

Related to cost monitoring and control:
1. Have any significant pricing changes occurred during the timeframe of the project?
2. Are there new opportunities to deliver the same or better project quality at a lower cost?

## Cost Control

Update the budget you created in Step 19 as you progress through the project. Budgeting is important for your project because it provides the basis for project cost control. By measuring the project's actual cost against the approved budget, you can determine if the project is progressing according to the plan or if corrective action is needed. This is accomplished using a cost baseline (Step 26).

## Earned Value

At this time, I wanted to introduce *Earned value (EV)*. It is one of the most sophisticated and accurate methods for measuring and controlling project schedules and budgets. Although it is sophisticated and used primarily in large projects, EV can be scaled to be appropriate for any size of the project. Other methods for measuring budget and schedules generally only monitor the percent of the time through the schedule and make the often mistaken assumption that this is also the percent that the project should be through the budget. But cost and schedule project progress generally are not evenly expended through a project. EV accurately deals with this reality.

In order to employ earned value, we must have a baseline plan (including a detailed, workload leveled, project schedule) in place that will allow us to continuously measure seven points of data. We must know what the "planned value" is as at any point in time.

To determine the **planned value**, we need to calculate two important base factors, 1) how much physical or intellectual work we have scheduled to be completed as of the point of measurement, and 2) what was the budgeted value of the work scheduled.

To measure **earned value** we need two new points of data: 3) how much of our scheduled work have we actually accomplished? And 4) what is the budgeted value of the work actually performed?

The next item is for the earned value of work we have accomplished, what 5) actual costs have we actually spent and/or incurred.

Next, we need to understand 6) the "schedule variance" which in earned value is the difference between our planned value scheduled and our earned value achieved.

Lastly, we need to know 7) what our "cost variances" have been. This is determined by relating our earned value accomplished against the actual costs spent or incurred.

These are the basics. Once armed with the EV information, the project manager and stakeholders can truly understand the current status of a project, the rates of variances, and once significantly into the project, accurately predict the end schedule and budget compared to the original estimates.

Please review the following Earned Value acronyms and formulas and then apply these formulas in the Earned Value Drill that follows the formulas.

| CV = EV - AC<br>(cost variance = earned value – actual cost) | Positive is GOOD. Negative is BAD. |
|---|---|
| CPI = EV / AC<br>(cost performance index = earned value / actual cost) | CPI of 1 means exactly on budget. Less than 1 means over budget (poor efficiency in the management of budget) Greater than 1 means under budget or high efficiency in the use of funds. |
| SV = EV - PV<br>(schedule variance = earned value – planned value) | Positive is GOOD. Negative is BAD. |
| SPI = EV / PV<br>(schedule performance index = earned value / planned value) | SPI of 1 means exactly on schedule. A SPI that is greater than 1 means better performance than plan. A SPI that is less than 1 means the project is not performing as well as originally planned. |
| ETC = EAC - AC<br>(estimate at completion = estimate at completion – actual cost) | The Estimate to Complete is the remaining amount of funds estimated to be needed from the reporting date to the end. |
| Percent Complete = EV / BAC * 100 (percent to complete = earned value / budget at completion * 100) ||
| VAC = BAC - EAC (variance at completion = budget at completion – estimate at completion) ||
| EV = % complete * BAC (earned value = % complete * budget at completion) ||
| % SPENT = AC / BAC * 100 (% spent = actual cost / budget at completion * 100) ||

# Earned Value Drill

Complete the chart below.

| BCWP (EV) | BCWS (PV) | ACWP (AC) | AHEAD OF SCHEDULE | BEHIND SCHEDULE | COST UNDERRUN | COST OVERRUN |
|---|---|---|---|---|---|---|
| 7000 | 9000 | 7000 |  | -2000 | 0 | 0 |
| 7000 | 6000 | 5000 | 1000 |  | 2000 |  |
| 3000 | 3000 | 6000 | 0 | 0 |  | -3000 |
| 5000 | 7000 | 6000 |  |  |  |  |
| 7000 | 8000 | 7000 |  |  |  |  |
| 9000 | 6000 | 8000 |  |  |  |  |
| 4000 | 3000 | 5000 |  |  |  |  |
| 6000 | 7000 | 5000 |  |  |  |  |
| 2000 | 3000 | 4000 |  |  |  |  |
| 8000 | 6000 | 6000 |  |  |  |  |
| 7000 | 9000 | 9000 |  |  |  |  |
| 5000 | 5000 | 8000 |  |  |  |  |
| 5000 | 4000 | 3000 |  |  |  |  |
| 9000 | 7000 | 8000 |  |  |  |  |
| 5000 | 5000 | 5000 |  |  |  |  |
| 8000 | 9000 | 7000 |  |  |  |  |
| 5000 | 4000 | 6000 |  |  |  |  |
| 9000 | 7000 | 7000 |  |  |  |  |
| 1000 | 2000 | 2000 |  |  |  |  |

See Answer Key

# 45. Manage Stakeholders – Monitor Engagement

*Maps to PMBOK 6th Edition*
*Process 13.4 Monitor Stakeholder Engagement*

The project manager must communicate with stakeholders to inform, resolve issues, and set accurate expectations. This is especially important whenever there are problems on the project.

The following is a checklist provided by Eric Verzuh, author of *The Fast Forward MBA in Project Management, Second Edition.*

- ☐ The project sponsor is fully aware of the state of the project, including revised schedule and budget estimates.
- ☐ The customer is fully aware of the state of the project, including revised schedule and budget estimates.
- ☐ The project team is fully aware of the state of the project, including revised schedule and budget estimates.
- ☐ Team members understand their specific assignments and how they fit into the overall project.
- ☐ Part-time team members and support organizations within the firm understand their contribution to the project. These expectations are clearly communicated both well in advance and again just prior to their involvement in order to give them the opportunity to plan to meet these expectations.
- ☐ The responsibility matrix is accurate.
- ☐ All stakeholders who need to be informed of project progress have adequate access to project information.

# CLOSING

At the end of a phase or project, you will need to close out the project activities which includes any contracts, reassigning resources and final project documentation.

## 46. Procurement Audits

The project manager must lead the responsibility of inspecting and identifying any weaknesses in the seller's work processes or deliverables.

## 47. Product Verification

Evaluating a deliverable at the end of a project or project phase with the intent to assure or confirm that it satisfies the planned intent.

Review the final project WBS and validate that everything planned was included. This is often done immediately before the formal acceptance.

## 48. Formal Acceptance

Note any required "punch list" of minor work that can be completed after formal project close-out.

Notes:

Acceptance:

_____
Sponsor Approval Signature                                        Date

# 49. Lessons Learned and Best Practices

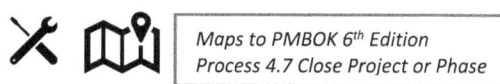

*Maps to PMBOK 6th Edition
Process 4.7 Close Project or Phase*

Start the *closure meeting* by presenting the factual project information, including the project name, project dates, names of the project manager and core team members, the baseline project plan, and the final project information. Then discuss the project report card.

**Sample Project Report Card**

| Review of the Completed Project | Notes | Grade Ranking (A – F) |
|---|---|---|
| How much did the project schedule vary from the original plan? What were the main factors that contributed towards variance? | | |
| How much did the actual cost vary from the original budget? | | |
| Grade the final performance/specification/grade and quality level. | | |
| Did the sponsor accept the final project? Did they think the process went well, that expectations were set accurately, and that they would commend the PM and team for a job well done? | | |
| Was the project completed with minimal, mutually agreed upon, scope changes? | | |
| Was the project performed without disturbing the main workflow of the organization? | | |
| Was the project completed without going against the corporate culture? | | |

## Lessons Learned Questions

To help facilitate your lessons learned meeting, here are some questions that may help generate constructive conversation.

1. What was the single most frustrating part of our project?

2. Are you proud of our finished deliverables (project work products)? If yes, what's so good about them? If no, what's wrong with them?

3. Describe any training and skill development that should be considered for our team to be better prepared for this type of project in the future.

4. Describe why the project was completed under, within, or over budget.

5. How should the project management process be improved in the future?

6. Provide a description of the major risks identified for the project and how they were handled.

7. How was change management handled during this project? What were the major project changes that occurred?

8. Was the communication process effective? Were there any major areas of misunderstandings or miscommunications during the project?

9. In hindsight, were there any topics that would have been helpful to have communicated much earlier in the project?

10. If you could wave a magic wand and change anything about the project, what would you change?

11. How were expectations related to the delivered product or service different than expected?

12. What is the primary lesson learned on this project?

See Appendix A - Templates

## Building Organizational Process Assets

The goal for collecting lessons learned is to share them with the organization to help future projects. Ask these two questions often to improve organizational processes:

1. How can the organization better share the project lessons learned?

2. How can the organization better collect and organize best practices?

# Common Lessons Learned from Unsuccessful Projects

Below are some common reasons that projects fail. Are there any you can add?

| | | | |
|---|---|---|---|
| **Keep reminders of old lessons learned nearby.** | Insufficient use of project/status reports | Meandering project attention | Inadequate project management, administrative, human & technical skills |
| | Insufficient project manager influence and authority | Poor coordination with client | Lack of rapport with client/parent organization |
| | Client disinterest in budget criteria | Lack of project team participation in decision making/Problem solving | Excessive structure within the project team |
| | Job insecurity within the project team | Lack of team spirit and sense of mission within the project team | Planning based on insufficient data |
| | A new type of project | Project more complex than handled previously (too complex) | Initial underfunding/ under-resourcing |
| | Inability to freeze design early | Inability to close out effort | Unrealistic project schedules |
| | Inadequate change procedures | Problem not clearly defined | Planning just performed by the planning group |
| | No one is in charge | Project estimates are best guesses, made without consulting historic data | People are constantly pulled off project or reassigned with no regard for the impact |
| | People don't see themselves working as one team | Ballpark estimates become official targets | The project plan lacks detail |
| | The project is not tracked to plan | People lose sight of the original goal | Resource planning is inadequate |
| | Use of superficial status reports | Senior managers refuse to accept reality | Blockages went unaddressed |
| | 90% done syndrome | We had a hammer and we made the project our nail. | Team members didn't follow instructions. |
| **Add new lessons here.** | | | |
| | | | |
| | | | |
| | | | |

## 50-51. Update Records and Archive Records

Documenting final information pertaining to acceptance documentation, project files, closure documents, and lessons learned is important. This often includes the completion of any needed compliance documentation. Archiving may involve putting the updated project records into a long-term storage location for later retrieval as needed.

If you have been tracking these, review the list of "Out of Scope" work and forward it with recommendations when appropriate. Also, review the "Wish List for Future Projects" and communicate it for consideration for future project selections.

## 52. Release Team

Acknowledgment and communication that the project team members have completed the required project work and that their services will no longer be required for this project. Often this is a point of recognition of the individual team member contributions, appreciation of their efforts, performance reporting, and transition to other activities.

**Show Gratitude**

Now is a time to encourage and congratulate team members. Consider sending thank you notes as an effective way to raise team morale and encourage strong and consistent ownership of new projects. A simple "thank you" with sincere praise and gratitude can do wonders in enhancing a team member's confidence and level of job satisfaction.

**Sample Thank You Letter**

Subject: Thank You for Your Hard Work

Dear Jane,

I really appreciate the effort you put in on the XYZ project. Our deadlines were challenging, and I know you put in a lot of extra time and went above and beyond the call of duty. Your effort truly helped to ensure that we met our deadlines.

Thank you so much for contributing your talents and skills to the team.

Sincerely,

Renee

# Glossary of Project Management Terms and Acronyms

## Acronyms

**CISD**: Critical Incident Stress Debriefing
**ERP**: Enterprise Resource Planning
**FUD**: Fear, Uncertainty, and Doubt
**PBS**: Product Breakdown Structure
**PM**: Project Management or Project Manager
**PMI**: Project Management Institute
**PMBOK**: A Guide to the Project Management Body of Knowledge®
**PMO**: Project Management Office
**PMP**: Project Management Professional
**RAM**: Responsibility Assignment Matrix
**RACI**: Responsible, Accountable, Consulted, Informed
**SME**: Subject Matter Expert. (See consult with SME's below.)
**SOW**: Statement of Work
**WBS**: Work Breakdown Structure (see below)

## Glossary

**8/80 Rule:** Although this is named a rule, it really isn't one – it is an occasionally used guideline that suggests that work packages in a WBS should be decomposed to equate to no more than 80 hours and no less than 8 hours of work. This guideline should be subordinate to the more appropriate guideline that the WBS should be decomposed to work packages at the level to which the work will be delegated.

**Acquire Resources:** The processes of obtaining team members, facilities, equipment, material and supplies necessary to complete the project work. In a matrix environment, this often involves working with functional managers to help establish team member availability, skills, interests, and administrative actions required. See section 9.3 of the PMBOK.

**Actual Cost (AC):** The costs actually incurred for the work completed by the specified date.

**Agile Project Management:** Agile project management has six principles and five phases. The principles are 1) deliver customer value, 2) employ interactive, feature-based delivery, 3) champion technical excellence, 4) encourage exploration, 5) build adaptive teams, and 6) simplify. The five phases are envision, speculate, explore, adapt, and close. Adherents of agile often believe it is a cultural phenomenon whose tenets are based more on chaos theory than didactic project management techniques.

**Analogous Estimating:** This form of estimating is very high-level and done quickly. It uses general experience with similar work to predict the time or cost of similar work in the future. It is often stated as "This is similar to something we have done in the past. That took X amount of time and cost. This is a little bigger than that – so it will probably be about 15% longer and more expensive."

**Apportioning:** Apportioning begins with a total project estimate, then assigns a percentage of that total to each of the phases and subprojects or work packages.

**Approach Analysis:** The work of consideration of alternative ways for how to technically or logistically achieve the project goals. This usually is performed during the planning phase. Approach analysis varies greatly depending on the type of project and the organization.

**Archive Records:** Putting the updated project records into a long-term storage location for later retrieval as needed.

**Assign a PM:** The initiation process step of naming a project manager to lead the project responsibilities on behalf of the project sponsor. This is ideally done before a project charter is announced.

**Baseline Project Plan:** This is the initial, approved project plan which usually includes a work breakdown structure, schedule, budget, and plan for how the resources, quality, risk, communication, procurement will be handled. See section 4.2.3.1 of the PMBOK.

**Bottom-Up Estimating:** This is the most accurate approach to project estimating. The process involves decomposing a project WBS into clear and assignable work packages and then gathering estimates for each work package from the responsible party. This form of estimating takes considerable time and effort; therefore, it often is not available during the early planning processes.

**Brook's Law:** The complexity and communications of a project rise geometrically with the number of team members, expressed as $[n(n-1)]/2$ where n equals the number of team members. The law is named after Dr. Fred Brooks and named after his book *The Mythical Man-Month*.

**Budget:** Generally, the sponsor-approved total cost baseline for a project. This often includes the estimated amount plus any approved project contingency and management reserves. See section 7.3 of the PMBOK.

**Burst Point:** A point in the project network diagram where when one task is complete many other tasks can begin. This is an important time for project managers to focus on project communications. It is a good time for team meetings.

**Change Control Plan:** Deciding what the processes will be for handling project changes that occur after the baseline plan is created until the end of the project. This usually includes informing team members and sponsors what the processes are for identifying, approving or rejecting changes to the project, recording the changes, and integrating them into the project plan. See section 4.6 of the PMBOK.

**Code of Accounts:** The ID system used in work breakdown structures and other configuration management documentation during the project management process (e.g.: a common level 3 work package code of accounts would be 1.1.3).

**Communication Plan:** This involves determining the information and communication needs of the project stakeholders. This usually includes planning how project status will be reported, how meetings will be conducted, and who needs what information. The project communication plan often needs to evolve during the project. See section 10.1 of the PMBOK.

**Complete Work Packages:** This is executing the work of the project. This is the effort of creating the project deliverables as scoped in the project work breakdown structure.

**Consult with SME's:** The input of subject matter experts (SME's) is greatly valued in project management. Getting the input, advice, and recommendations from technical and industry experts should be a step performed by the project manager during the project planning phase.

**Contingency:** Contingencies are also called buffers, reserves, or padding. They are the funds or time needed above the initial estimate to reduce the risk to an acceptable level. It is important to include contingencies in the project estimates.

**Contract Administration:** The work of managing the agreement and performance between the buyer and the vendor/seller. This also involves managing contract-related changes. See section 12.3 of the PMBOK.

**Cost Budgeting:** See the definition for budget.

**Cost Monitoring and Control:** The work of gathering and reporting information on the project costs, managing the changes as they occur, and acting to bring any potential cost overruns into acceptable limits. See section 7.4 of the PMBOK.

**Cost Performance Index (CPI):** The ratio of the approved budget for work performed to what you actually spent for the work. The CPI reflects the relative value of work done compared to the amount paid for it, sometimes referred to as the project's cost efficiency. You can use the CPI to date to project the cost performance for the remainder of the task.

**Cost Variance (CV):** The difference between the amount budgeted and the amount actually spent on the work performed. The CV shows whether and by how much you're under or over your approved budget.

**Crashing:** The technique of speeding up the project schedule by using more resources (i.e.: people, materials, or equipment) than what was originally planned.

**Critical Path:** The series of activities that determines the duration of the project. The critical path is usually defined as those activities with no slack. It is the longest path through the project.

**Customer/Sponsor:** The individual or group that has requested or who is paying for the project. This could be an internal department, someone in management, or an external organization or person.

**Decomposition:** Decomposition involves subdividing the major project deliverables into smaller, more manageable components until the deliverables are defined in sufficient detail to support future project activities (planning, executing, controlling, and closing).

**Deliverable:** Any measurable, tangible, verifiable outcome, result, or item that must be produced to complete a project or part of a project. Often used more narrowly in reference to an external deliverable, which is a deliverable that is subject to approval by the project sponsor or customer.

**Develop Team:** Taking steps to improve the team interactions and skill competencies for the project. See section 9.4 of the PMBOK.

**Divide Large Projects into Phases:** The process of breaking large projects into a program of smaller time-based subprojects for the sake of better control.

**Earned value (EV):** The approved budget for the work actually completed by the specified date.

**Enterprise Resource Planning (ERP):** Integrated applications involving forecasting and planning, purchasing and material management, warehousing and inventory management, finished product distribution, accounting, and finance.

**Estimate at Completion (EAC):** Your estimate today of the total cost of the task

**Estimate to Complete (ETC):** Your estimate of the amount of funds required to complete all work still remaining to be done on the task

**Fast Track:** The technique of speeding up the project schedule by altering the planned schedule through doing work simultaneously that would have ideally been performed consecutively.

**Fallback Plan**: a plan for an alternative course of action that can be adopted to overcome the consequences of a risk, should it occur (including carrying out any advance activities that may be required to render the plan practical).

**Feasibility:** The project initiation step of determining that a project is likely to be completed successfully. It is often an evaluation that there are enough available financial resources, technology, or skills to meet the needs of the project. See section 4.1 of the PMBOK.

**Formal Acceptance:** Sponsor acknowledgment and approval of the final project deliverables. See section 4.7.1.4 of the PMBOK.

**Gantt Charts:** Bar charts that list all activities vertically with corresponding bars which visually display the planned timeframe for each of the activities by use of a hollow bar, which is shaded in as percentages of the activity are completed.

**Going Native:** Another possible pitfall of project groups is going native. This phenomenon can occur within project teams working off-site or when the project team becomes closely identified with the customer

**Grade:** A category or rank used to distinguish items that have the same functional use (e.g.: a Web site), but do not share the same requirements for quality (e.g.: different Web sites may have to provide much more functionality).

**Hammock:** A point in a project network diagram where many tasks feed into Task X, and then many other tasks can start as soon as Task X is complete. It is an important time for the project manager to schedule sponsor reviews and approvals. It may be a natural start for a new project phase.

**High Level Planning:** The work done during the project initiation phase that helps set the general approach to be used by a project team. This may include an analysis of various potential approaches and providing a high-level recommendation on a preferred way to approach achieving the project goals.

**Hypercritical Activities:** Activities on the critical path with negative float.

**Information Distribution:** This includes performing the communication management plan, often including providing project status reports and facilitating project meetings, as well as responding to unexpected requests for information. See section 10.2 of the PMBOK.

**Integrated Change Control:** This is the work of performing the project change management activities. The changes often occur at an unexpected time and require time to properly manage and integrate. See section 4.6 of the PMBOK.

**Ishikawa Diagram:** Sometimes called a fishbone diagram, this diagram is a problem-solving approach by Kaoru Ishikawa used to show how causes and sub-causes relate to cause possible problems or effects.

**Kubler-Ross Five Stages of Grief Model:** Named after Elisabeth Kubler-Ross, Swiss psychoanalyst, the model stages are denial, anger, bargaining, depression, and acceptance. Why is this in the project management glossary? This model often forms the underpinnings of organizational change (which projects often are involved with).

**Lessons Learned:** Documented and stored information pertaining to the continuous improvement suggestions for handling similar projects in the future.

**Loop:** A network path that passes the same node twice. Loops cannot be analyzed using traditional network analysis techniques and are treated as errors.

**Manage by Exception to the Project Plan:** This is based on a philosophy that the project baseline plan should be well-planned, clear and understandable to the project stakeholders. When questions arise the project plan should answer the most predictable questions. This frees the project manager to address the things that are differing from the baseline project plan – usually meaning they are spending most of their time managing the project changes to improve the project results.

**Manage Stakeholder Engagement:** Communicating to inform, resolve issues, and set accurate expectations with the people who have an interest in the project. See section 13.3 of the PMBOK.

**Manage Team:** Tracking team member performance, providing feedback, resolving issues, and coordinating changes to enhance the project performance. It usually involves communicating both formally and informally with team members and managing conflicts. See section 9.5 of the PMBOK.

**Manage Quality:** This involves the work of applying the quality plan, or more specifically to ensure that the project has the necessary quality tools and techniques, performing quality audits, and analyzing the processes. The results of quality assurance include making improvements to the project deliverables, processes, and/or plan. See section 8.2 of the PMBOK.

**Management Reserve:** A financial or schedule reserve, or buffer, that is available to the project, but that the project manager must get permission to utilize. This reserve is for "unknown unknowns" unlike the project contingency, which is for "known unknowns".

**Milestone:** A significant event in the project, usually completion of a major deliverable.

**Mind Mapping:** Nonlinear diagramming of words, ideas, or topics around the main concept. This was popularized by Tony Buzan, who reportedly developed the concept because he studied the notebooks of Leonardo da Vinci.

**Modern Project Management (MPM):** A term used to distinguish the current broad range of project management (scope, cost, time, quality, risk, etc.) from narrower, traditional use that focused on cost and time.

**Moses Factor:** When a group subconsciously follows a charismatic leader and adopts their preferred risk attitude, even when it may contradict the personal preferences of individual group preferences.

**Near-Critical Activity:** An activity that has a low total float.

**Network Diagram:** Any schematic display of the logical relationships of project activities. Always drawn from left to right to reflect project chronology (like a flowchart). Often referred to as a PERT Chart. Network diagrams should show the critical path of a project. The following information should be shown for each work package: the name or ID, early start date, duration, early finish date, the late start date, slack time, and late finish date. See Step 16 Network Diagramming in this workbook for instructions on how to create network diagrams.

**Order of Magnitude Estimate:** An initial, broad estimate with a broad accuracy range. It has been defined in previous PMBOK versions as +/-50%, but much of the industry defines it as +75% to -25% accuracy.

**Parametric Estimate:** An estimating technique that relies on quantifying the project scope through metrics. For example, the cost may be based on a set cost per foot, per minute, per unit, etc.

**Performance Reporting:** This involves collecting and distributing performance information on the project status (often including schedule, budget, quality, risk, and team performance information). This often also includes using the status information to forecast future results. See section 10.3 of the PMBOK.

**PERT Estimate:** The practice of basing an estimate on the calculation of three scenarios including a pessimistic scenario (P), most-likely (ML), and optimistic (O) scenario. The formula is generally calculated as $(P + 4ML + O)/6$.

**Planned Value (PV):** The approved budget for the work scheduled to be completed by a specified date.

**Preliminary Project Scope Statement:** A high-level initial description of the work and/or deliverables that are intended to be included in the new project. This is usually preliminary during the initiation phase and it becomes more well-defined during the planning phase. See the contents of the project charter which includes a high-level project description in section 4.1 in the PMBOK.

**Procurement Audits:** The buyers work of inspecting and identifying any weaknesses in the seller's work processes or deliverables. See section 12.3 of the PMBOK.

**Procurement Plan:** Determining the approach that will be used for purchasing outside products and services for the project. See section 12.1.3 of the PMBOK.

**Product Breakdown Structure (PBS):** A hierarchy of deliverable products which are required to be produced on the project. It forms the base document from which the execution strategy and product-based work breakdown structure may be derived. It provides a guide for configuration control documentation.

**Product Verification:** Evaluating a deliverable at the end of a project or project phase with the intent to assure or confirm that it satisfies the planned intent. This is often done immediately before the formal acceptance. See section 4.7 in the PMBOK.

**Program:** A group of related projects managed in a coordinated way. Programs usually include an element of ongoing work.

**Project:** A temporary endeavor undertaken to create a unique product, service, or result.

**Project Charter:** A document issued by senior management that formally authorizes the existence of a project. It provides the project manager with the authority to apply organizational resources to project activities. Read more about charters in the PMBOK section 4.1.

**Project Contingency:** A financial or schedule reserve, or buffer, that is available to the project, but may not have to be used. This reserve is for "known unknowns" (such as an artistic redesign if the client doesn't like the first draft) unlike the management contingency, which is for "unknown unknowns".

**Project Cost Management:** A subset of project management that includes the processes required to ensure that the project is completed within the approved budget. It consists of resource planning, cost estimating, cost budgeting, and cost control.

**Project Life Cycle:** A collection of generally sequential project phases whose name and number are determined by the control needs of the organization or organizations involved in the project.

**Project Management:** The application of knowledge, skills, tools and techniques to project activities to meet the project requirements.

**Project Selection Methods:** The organization's techniques for selecting which projects get chartered. (Recommended reading: Chapter 2 of the *Project Management Toolbox by Dragan Z. Milosevic.*)

**Quality Assurance:** This involves the work of applying the quality plan, or more specifically to ensure that the project has the necessary quality tools and techniques, performing quality audits, and analyzing the processes. The results of quality assurance include making improvements to the project deliverables, processes, and/or plan. See section 8.2 of the PMBOK.

**Quality Control (QC):** Identifying and implementing ways to eliminate unsatisfactory results. This often includes prevention efforts, attribute sampling, identifying the causes of problems, defining acceptable and unacceptable variances, and managing defect repair. See section 8.3 of the PMBOK.

**Quality Plan:** The work of determining what quality standards will be important to the stakeholders of the project and coming up with plans to satisfy them. (Recommended reading: *Managing Quality – An Integrative Approach.*) See section 8.1 in the PMBOK.

**Release Team:** Acknowledgement and communication that the project team members have completed the required temporary work and that their services will no longer be required for this project. Often this is a point of recognition of the individual team member contributions, appreciation of their efforts, performance reporting, and transition to other activities.

**Request Seller Responses:** This is a step when buying products and/or services from vendors/sellers. It is the work of requesting bids and proposals. See section 12.2 of the PMBOK.

**Resource Identification:** The step of listing the people, equipment, and materials that are expected to be needed for the project. The outcome of resource identification is often a printed Resource Breakdown Structure (RBS).

**Resource Management Plan:** The process of identifying and documenting project roles, responsibilities and reporting relationships. This often includes coordinating with functional managers and the process of creating a responsibility assignment matrix (RAM). See section 9.1 in the PMBOK.

**Responsibility Assignment Matrix (RAM) also often referred to as RACI for Responsible, Accountable, Consulted, and Informed:** A table form that relates the project team structure to the areas of work of the project to help ensure that all of the responsibility roles are understood.

**Risk Categories:** High-level groupings (such as safety, equipment, weather) used for aiding accurate risk identification. Categories should be well defined and should reflect common sources of risk for the industry or application area.

**Risk Plan:** The process of deciding how to approach and conduct the risk management activities of a project. See section 11.1 of the PMBOK.

**Risk Response:** The work of developing options and to determine how to enhance opportunities and reduce threats to the project. See section 11.6 of the PMBOK.

**Schedule Control:** The work of determining the current schedule status, influencing the factors that might affect the schedule, determining when a schedule change has occurred and managing the schedule changes as they do occur. See section 6.6 of the PMBOK.

**Schedule Performance Index (SPI):** The ratio of the approved budget for the work performed to the approved budget for the work planned. The SPI reflects the relative amount the project is ahead of or behind schedule, sometimes referred to as the project's schedule efficiency. You can use the SPI to date to project the schedule performance for the remainder of the task.

**Schedule Variance (SV):** The difference between the amounts budgeted for the work you actually did and for the work you planned to do. The SV shows whether and by how much your work is ahead of or behind your approved schedule.

**Scheduling:** Setting the project plan dates for executing project work and achieving project milestones. See section 6.5 of the PMBOK.

**Scope:** The sum of the products, services, and results to be provided as a project.

**Scope Control:** The work of influencing the factors that create project scope changes and controlling the impact of those changes. This includes noticing when changes are occurring, filtering out changes from inappropriate people, and ensuring that changes that are accepted into the project are beneficial. See section 5.6 of the PMBOK.

**Scope Statement:** Usually a written document describing the project business purpose, objectives and goals, and scope. It often is begun in the project initiation phase (as a preliminary scope statement) and further evolves with the project planning. It is often similar (at least initially) to the project charter. See section 5.3 in the PMBOK for more information.

**Scrum:** A project approach first described by Hirotaka Takeuchi and Ikujiro Nonaka in their Harvard Business Review Article *"The New New Product Development Game"* (1986). Today it is one of the widely used agile methods that accept that the development process is unpredictable. The term is borrowed from the game of rugby.

**Select Vendors:** This is the work of evaluating vendors/sellers ability to provide the requested products and/or services. Specifically, this relates to the final decision and negotiation involved with coming to the purchasing agreement contract.

**Sink Point:** A point in a network diagram where multiple tasks converge into one. This usually is a high-risk time for the project schedule. This is a time when the project manager should focus on quality and project control.

**Soft Project:** A project that is intended to bring about change and does not have a physical product.

**Solicit Stakeholder Input:** The step of gathering input from various project stakeholders is often done during the project planning phase. This may take the form of interviews, surveys, or other information gathering techniques.

**Stakeholder Analysis:** The step of identifying and considering the interests of the various potential project customers and other individuals and organizations who will potentially be affected by your project. It is recommended that a stakeholder analysis is done during the initiation phase. Actually, soliciting the input of stakeholders often occurs slightly later, during the project planning phase. See Step 5 Stakeholder Analysis in this workbook for further information and a stakeholder identification brainstorming sheet. See section 13.1 in the PMBOK for an excellent business case for doing stakeholder analysis.

**Statement of Work (SOW):** A narrative description of products or services to be supplied under the contract.

**Sunk Costs:** Past costs in a project that can never be recovered. It is strongly suggested that sunk costs should not be considered a factor in deciding whether to terminate a project or allow it to continue to the next phase.

**Time and Cost Estimating:** Making decisions regarding the duration of work or the financial resources required for a project (or individual tasks in a project) based on the best available information. This is required for schedule and budget creation. It is usually done during the planning phase and refined during the control and monitoring phase. For more information see *"Project Management: A Systems Approach to Planning, Scheduling, and Controlling"* by Harold Kerzner. In chapter 14 he discusses Pricing and Estimating. Also, see section 6.4 in the PMBOK.

**Time Box:** A set time in which an activity, task, iteration, or other effort must be completed. Used in agile software development methods to fix the amount of time devoted to developing a particular iteration. Once the time box is closed, work stops and whatever was developed is used for the next step in the process. Sometimes called "time boxing".

**Tornado Diagrams:** A type of bar chart where the bars are sorted from widest on top down to smallest. They are useful for comparing the importance of variables. The PMBOK references tornado diagrams as a tool for sensitivity analysis associated with Quantitative Risk Analysis and Modeling Techniques. See Figure 11-14: Example Tornado Diagram, in PMBOK.

**True-Up:** To make balanced or to integrate plans. Used in project and program management as an expression meaning to bring into alignment with plans and processes.

**Update Records:** Documenting the final information pertaining to the acceptance documentation, project files, closure documents, and lessons learned. This often includes the completion of any needed compliance documentation. See section 4.7 of the PMBOK.

**Validate Scope:** The work of obtaining formal acceptance of the completed project deliverables. This usually involves some form of inspection. See section 5.5 of the PMBOK.

**WBS - Work Breakdown Structure:** The WBS is an outline of the work that is to be done to complete the project. It is a way to organize the project, it is the basis from which the project is controlled, and it ensures that the plan is complete. See the Project Management Institute's *Practice Standard for Work Breakdown Structures*.

**WBS Dictionary:** Work-package working instructions for the assigned party. This usually includes the time and budget allocated for this work.

**Workload Leveling:** The process of fitting the planned work into the availability of the resources assigned in a way that evens out the ups and downs of work performed and accommodates for the prior commitments of the team members. This generally has the effect of lengthening the project schedule and making it more realistic than a non-workload leveled schedule.

**Work Package:** A deliverable at the lowest level of the Work Breakdown Structure, when that deliverable may be assigned to another person.

# Answer Key

## Introduction

## Case Study: New Project at Global Green Books Publishing

*Global Green Books Publishing* was started two years ago by two friends, Jim King, and Brad Mount, who met in college while studying in Philadelphia, USA. In the new business, Jim focused on editing, sales, and marketing while Brad Mount did the electronic assembly and publishing of books for Global Green Books. Their business was successful and profitable in the first two years, largely due to contracts from two big businesses.

As the eBook business grew, there were more and more demands on the supervisors. Many were great print technicians who had caught the eye of the founders for their attitudes and customer service ethic. But today, they are being called on to do more complex tasks than merely running a highly automated print copier. Supervisors are interacting with customers, as well as with internal account managers and customer service representatives. They are managing employees with a diverse set of skills, backgrounds, and motivations.

In their third year, they got very busy thanks to their third major customer, a local college that needed customized eBooks. As a result, they hired Samantha as a project management assistant. In her new role as a project manager, she was to be assigned to this new project.

Global Green Books has been told by the college how many different printing jobs the college would need. Understanding what each eBook needed had to be clearly documented and understood before starting production.

Each e-book being produced was indeed a book, but that was all they had in common. Each book had different production steps, different contents and reprint approvals required, and different layouts and cover designs. Some were just collections of articles to reprint once approvals were received, and others required extensive desktop publishing. Each eBook was a complex process but was going to be made just once, as these eBooks were all customized for each professor and course each semester. Each eBook had to be produced on time and had to be made to match just exactly what the professors requested.

Each eBook will have a separate job order prepared that listed all the steps that needed to be completed so that tasks could be assigned to each worker and costs estimated.

For the purposes of this project, assume costs of 10,000. Global Green Books targets a 25% profit margin on each project, and budgets for a 10% contingency on labor and 20% contingency on permissions.

Credit to: PMITeach.org

# 1. Project Selection Methods

### Define these in your own words:

**Time Value of Money**: A dollar in your hand today is worth more than a dollar you will receive in the future because a dollar in hand today can be invested to turn into more *money* in the future.

**Opportunity Cost**: Refers to the value forgone in order to make one articular investment instead of another.

**Sunk Cost**: is a cost that has already been incurred and cannot be recovered.

## Net Present Value (NPV) Sample Problem

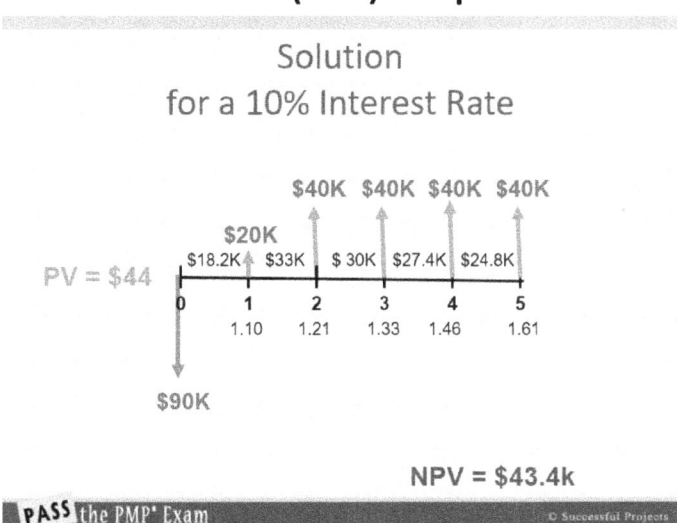

Let's use our visual timeline to build our answer. Start by drawing out 5 years on a timeline and indicate the $90K investment at the beginning. Then indicate the savings, above the line. We have the planned cost savings of $20K at the end of year one, and $40K at the end of each of the following years.

Then, let's add the interest, or time effect, to these forecasted savings. If the interest rate is 10% per year, it doesn't affect our initial investment of $90K. But after time starts passing, we calculate each year's effect by the number of the year plus the interest rate to the power of the number of years: $(1+r)^n$. For year 1 that factor is 1.1, for year 2 it is 1.21, for year 3 it is 1.33, year 4 it is 1.46, and for year 5 it is 1.61.

## NPV Sample Problem

Remember: The Present Value Formula is $FV/(1 + .10)^n$

| Year | FV | /Factor | Present Value |
|---|---|---|---|
| 0 | -$90k | /1 | -$90 |
| 1 | $20k | /1.10 | $18.2 |
| 2 | $40k | /1.21 | $33 |
| 3 | $40k | /1.33 | $30 |
| 4 | $40k | /1.46 | $27.4 |
| 5 | $40k | /1.61 | $24.8 |
|   |   |   | $43.4 |

We subtract the $90K and add the income for each year based on the savings divided by the Interest Factor, giving us the present value for the savings each year, which nets out at $43.4K.

*Assuming the cost of money is 10%, what would the NPV of this project be? NPV = 43.4K*

### Payback Period Sample Problem:
*Payback period = $50k/$35k = 1.43 yrs*

### Benefit / Cost Ratio Sample Problem:
*Benefit / Cost Ratio = ($40k * 5yr) / $100k = 2.0 or 2:1*

## 4. Assign a Project Manager

### Organizational Structure
*In the space below, draw an example of a Functional, Balanced Matrix and Project Oriented Hierarchical Organization Chart and indicate where the project manager would fall within each structure.*

See examples below of different organizational structures. You can also visit the link below for more information on the matrix organization. *https://www.pmi.org/learning/library/matrix-organization-structure-reason-evolution-1837*

## Functional

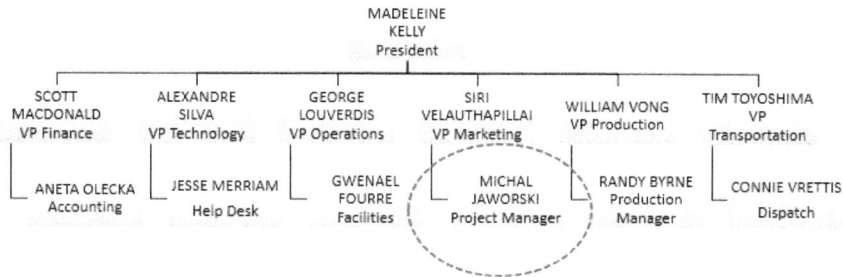

## Matrix

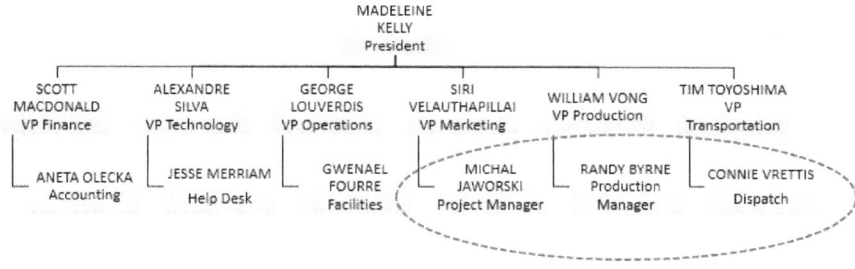

## Project Oriented

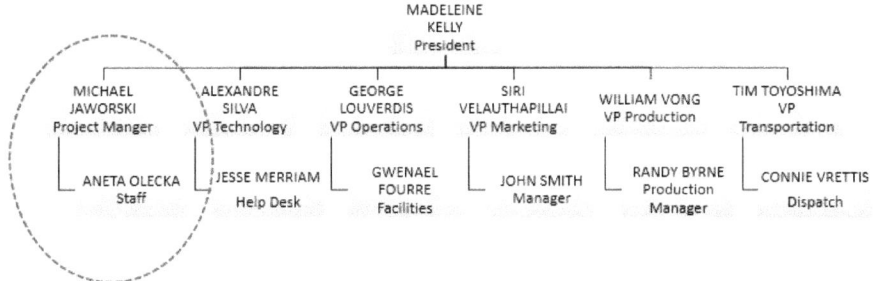

## 6. Project Charter

### Charter Questions
1. Who should send out your project charter? Project Sponsor

2. List the points you want to remember to include in your project charter, such as: High Level Project Description, Project Manager Name, High level – risks, assumptions, constraints, budget, a summary of the business case

3. Suggested distribution list for your charter: Project Sponsor, Project Team, Other Key Stakeholders


## 13. Create the Work Breakdown Structure (WBS)
**What are the benefits associated with developing and using a Work Breakdown Structure?**
The WBS defines 100% of what is included in the project. Therefore, it helps prevent scope creep. It also helps the team with estimating and seeing how their pieces of the project fit with others. Because it outlines 100% of the work, the WBS also helps to prevent work from slipping through the cracks.


## 16. Network Diagramming: Network Calculation Exercises

**Very Easy**

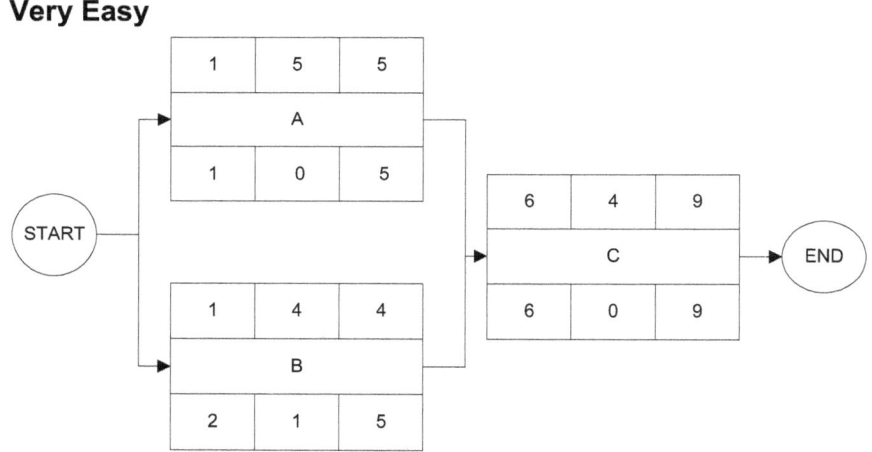

**Easy**

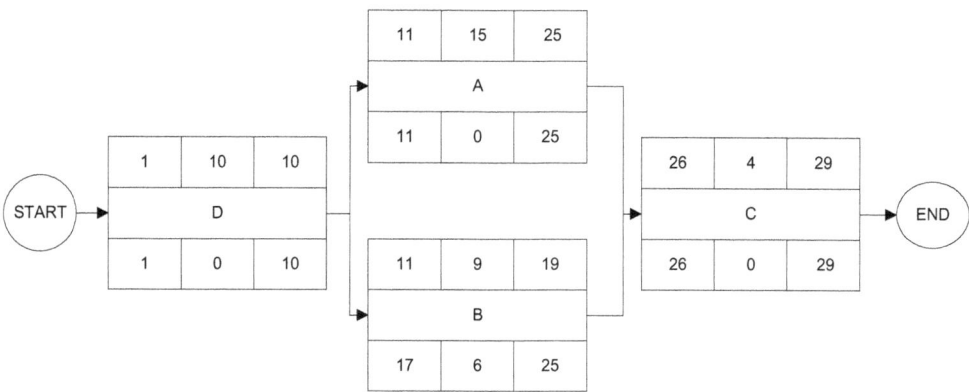

**Moderate**

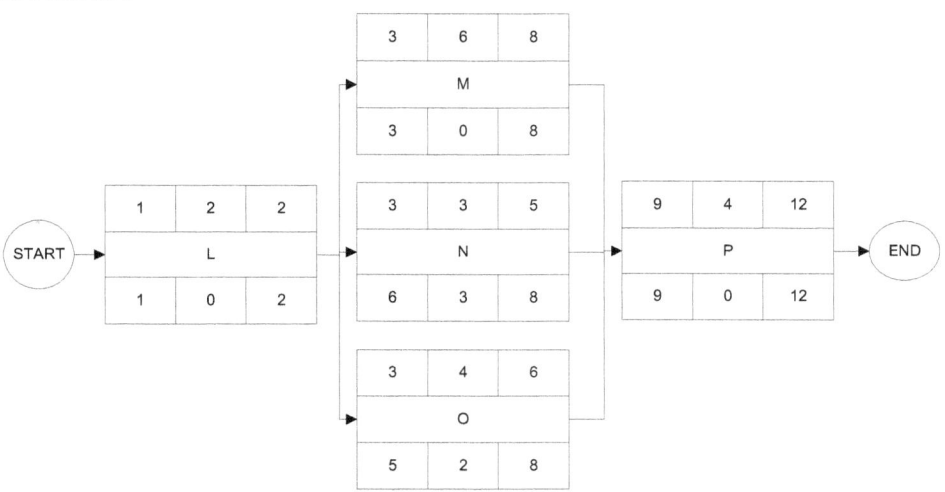

## Difficult

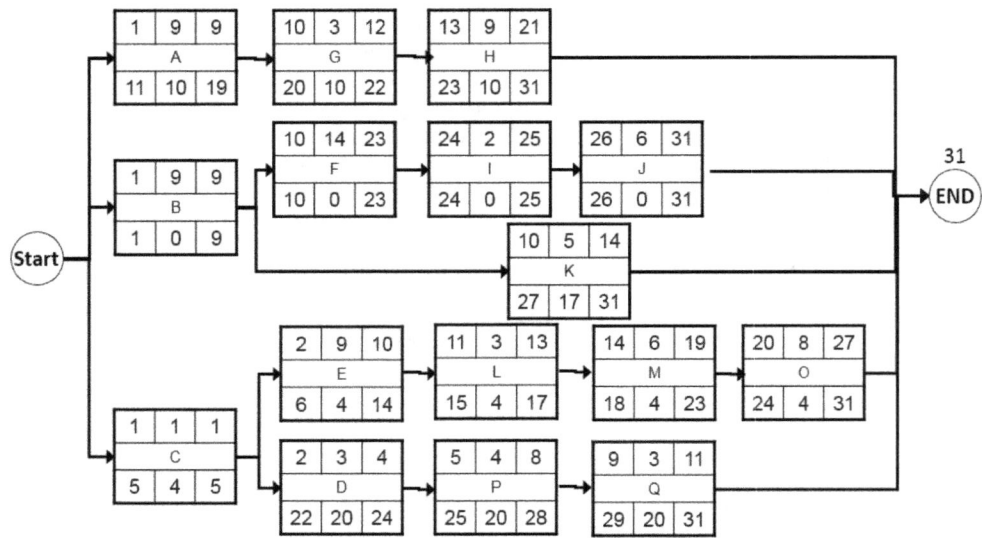

## Network Diagrams to Calculate from Tables:

### Project A

**On Project A**, the critical path was ACFHI. The duration was 21. Activity B's float is impacted due to the start-to-start relationship with D. There is potential that B could start just enough to start D, and then it could utilize its float before finishing.

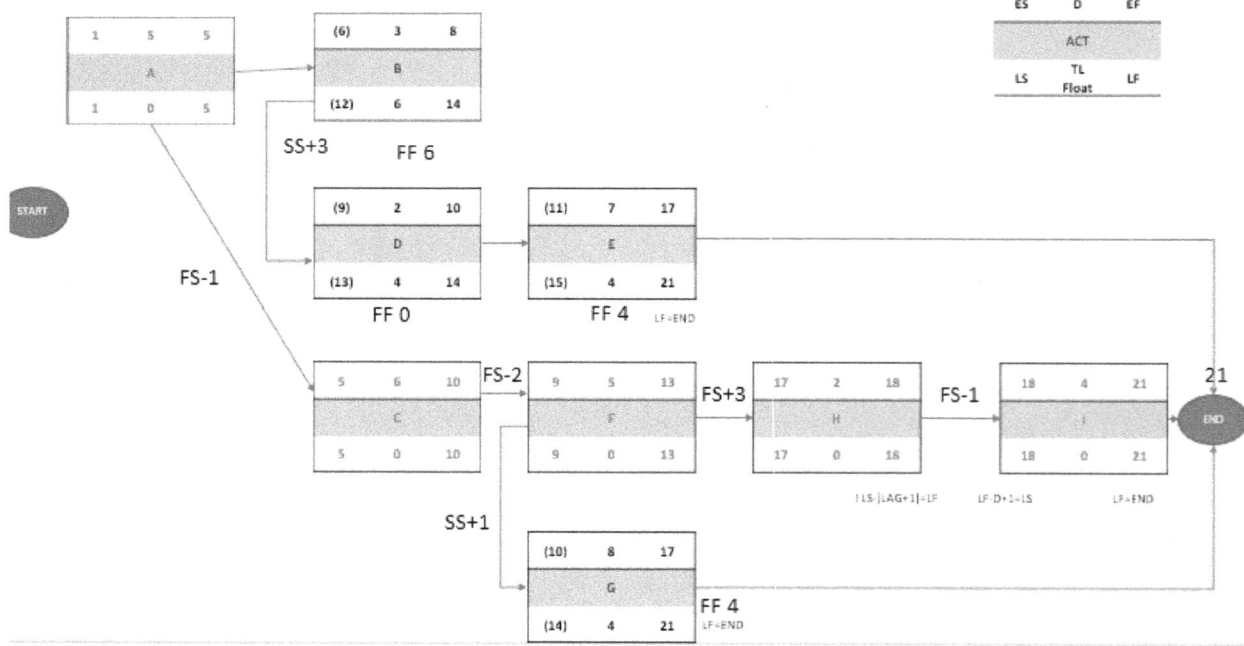

# Project B

**On Project B,** the critical path was CFG and it had a duration of 32.

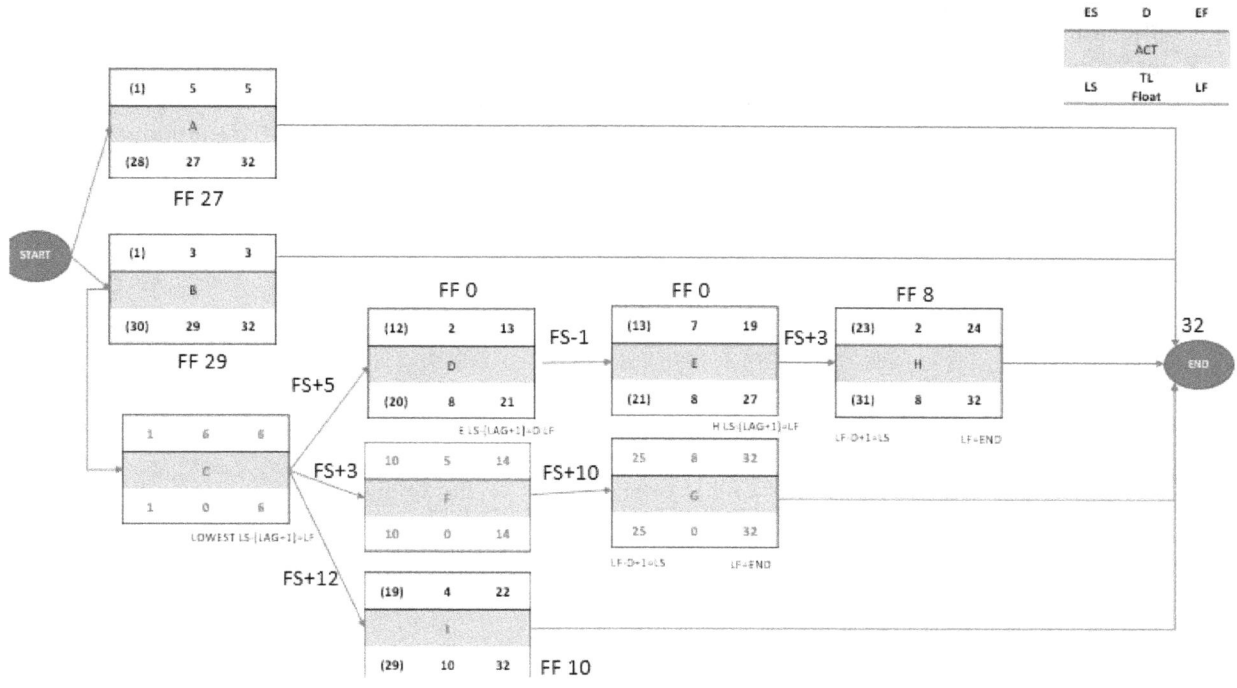

## Project C

**On project C,** the critical path is ABCDE with a duration of 65. You will note that the S-S relationship of E to D again causes an issue with the late start of D – forcing it to be 50 (although the late finish may be 65 – therefore making the float hard to define and prone to allowing the activity to start and stop). The late start of E is 49 and its late finish is 65. Remember that the -1 indicates a lead between the S-S of D to E. It may seem strange that the dependency relationship of D to E has a lead - when it might have been done as an E to D dependency with a lag of 1 instead. But the dependency relationship given in a problem must be assumed to be correctly defined. It may help to think of a track relay race where the person grabbing the baton E starts running to gain speed before D can pass the baton.

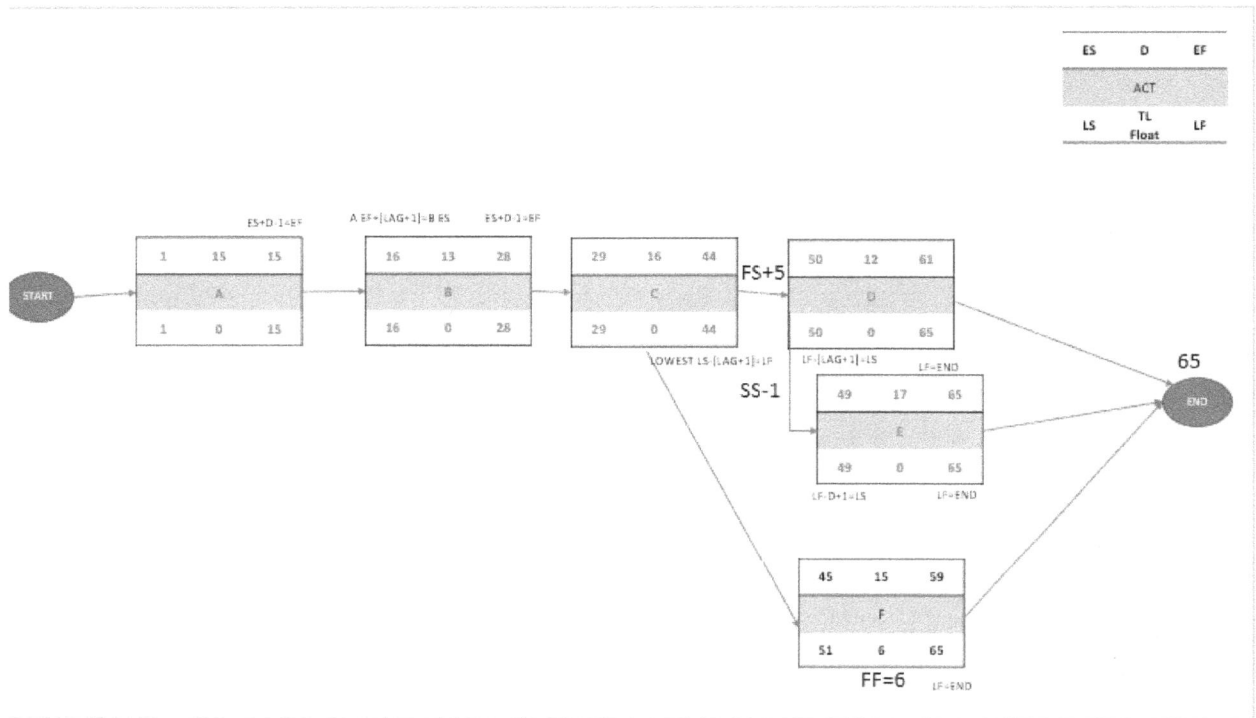

## 17-18. Scheduling and Workload Leveling

### Resource Optimization

#### Resource Leveling
Resource Leveling adjusts the start dates and finish dates of different activities in order to balance the demand for resources vs available supply.

#### Resource Smoothing
Resource smoothing is used to adjust the activities of a schedule so that requirements for the resources do not go beyond the resource's limits pre-defined during the planning.

## Schedule Compression

### Crashing

**Crashing** is a schedule compression technique where you add extra resources to the project to compress the schedule. In crashing, you review the critical path and see which activities can be completed by adding extra resources.

### Fast Tracking

In **fast tracking**, you review the critical path to find out which sequential activities can be performed parallel or partially parallel to each other. Fast tracking helps you reduce the duration of the schedule within limits. If you continue to fast track after this limit, it may increase the risk beyond acceptable levels and lead to possible rework or future delays.

## Practice Problem: Determining Mark's Project Work Completion

**Answer to Practice Problem: Determining Mark's Project Work Completion**

| # Day | 1 | 2 | 3 | 4 | 5 | 6 | 7 | 8 | 9 | 10 | 11 | 12 | 13 | 14 | 15 | 16 | 17 | 18 | 19 | 20 |
|---|---|---|---|---|---|---|---|---|---|---|---|---|---|---|---|---|---|---|---|---|
| Day of Week | Mon | Tues | Wed | Thur | Fri | Sat | Sun | Mon | Tues | Wed | Thur | Fri | Sat | Sun | Mon | Tues | Wed | Thur | Fri | Sat |
| Hours Mark Can Work | 3 | 3 | 6 | 6 | 6 | Off | Off | 6 | 6 | 6 | 6 | Vac | Off | Off | 6 | 6 | 6 | 6 | 6 | Off |
| Task Progress | Start 1 | End 1 | 2 | Lag | Lag | | | Lag | 3 | 4 | 5 | | | | 6 | 7 | | | | |

The answer is that Mark will be done on <u>Day 16</u>.
Here is the logic process used in deriving the answer:
Start by noting what days Mark doesn't work in the grid (the weekends and his planned vacation date).
Insert the number of hours per day that Mark expects he can work on your project.
Insert the tasks in the dates the work will start and end including the 3 days of lag between tasks 2 & 3.

# Making Smart Project Schedule Decisions

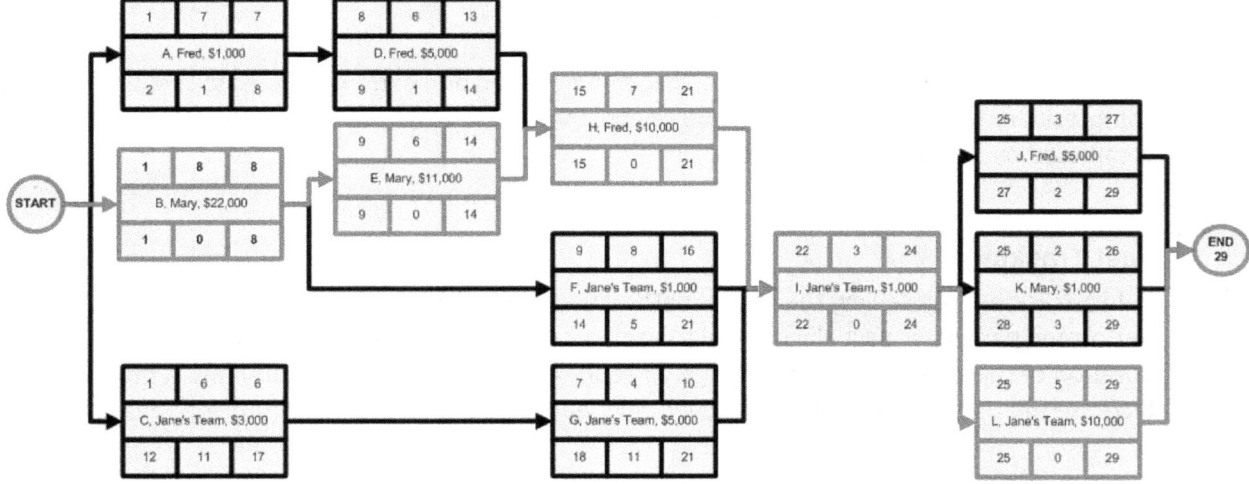

1. What activities create the project's critical path? *BEHIL*
2. What is G's slack time if C used 6 weeks of its available slack time?
   *The total float time is shared on the path. Your team members need to know that. So, when we start to dip into the float time already with activity C, the 6 weeks that they used is no longer available to G. They have only 5 of the total 11 weeks left to use now on G.*
3. During week 1, what activity is your greatest concern? *B as it is on the Critical Path*
4. If Jane and her Team can't do any work on this project during weeks 9 and 10, can we still work with them and achieve our schedule?
   *First, hopefully, you identified all of the activities planned for Jane's Team in this timeframe, which is C, F, and G. Then if you look at the float time, you see they can continue on schedule despite their constraint because they have enough float to work around that scheduling conflict.*
5. If you had to pick 4 milestone points in the project based on the network diagram, where would they fall?
   *Towards the beginning, the end of B is a milestone because it is a **burst point**. And it is the most expensive part of the project and it's on the critical path. The end of D/E may be a milestone because it is **a sink point** on the critical path. "I" could be a milestone either at its start or at its finish. But it's a small activity both in time and cost, so you wouldn't give it two milestone markers. The convention would tend to wrap it with the work before it and put the milestone at the end of I. But it could go either place.*
6. Assume you are the project manager and you want to take a 2-week vacation sometime during the project. When is the best time for you to be out on vacation? Does the network diagram or Gantt chart do a better job of helping you make this decision?

   *Gantt charts is a Stacked Bar Chart to represent Project Schedule in Graphical Representation. It does a good job of focusing on the scheduled dates. The Networks diagram is Flow Chart representation of sequential workflow of the Project Tasks. The Gantt chart would be a better option to see the best time to take vacation. I would recommend the*

*PM should try to take their vacation between weeks 21 ½ - 23 1/2, because nothing is starting or ending then – even if float time is used. The least amount of work is occurring, with only one activity in the process.*

7. Create a line chart of the cumulative planned project expenditures assuming work happens as soon as possible, and that billing is done upon completion of the activities.

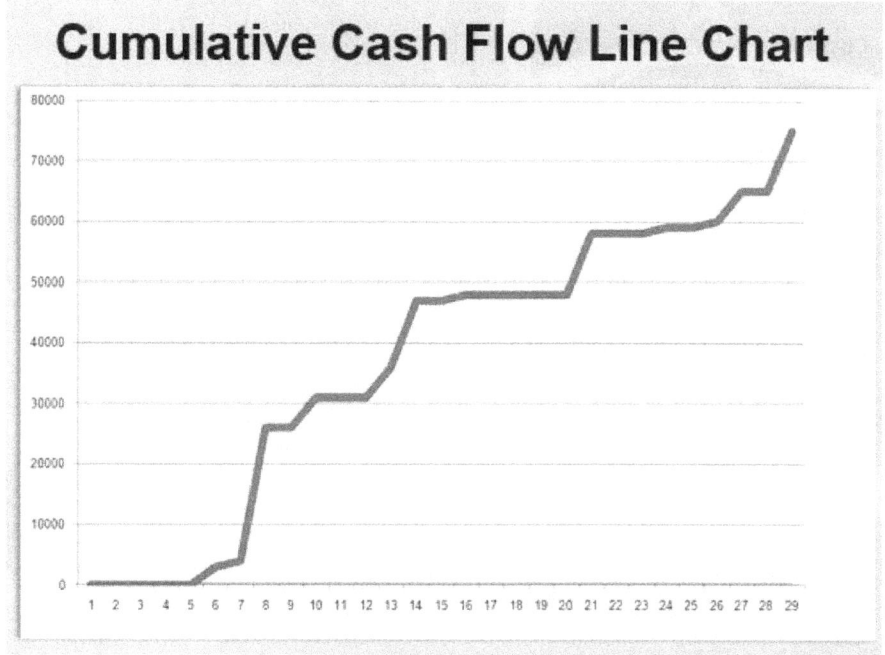

8. Compare and contrast the usefulness of the network diagram, Gantt chart, and line chart of expenditures.

   *A Line chart is good for showing trends such as expenditures over time, the Gantt chart shows the scheduled activities over time, and the network diagram shows the workflow.*

9. If the customer wants the project schedule shortened, what is the best activity to focus on shortening (crashing)? The second and third best? Remember that it only pays to crash the work that is on the critical path because the other work has float/slack time available.

   *The first criteria are that it has to be on the critical path. And you want to put the effort into shortening something that is not going to immediately bump the critical path off to another activity which is why you wouldn't select B or E (LOOK AT THE DURATION OF A,B,C ALL ARE VERY CLOSE 6,7,8). Then as you look at the remaining tasks, you try to find work that can be shortened quite a bit, but where it isn't a huge percentage of the duration– so look at the longer activities.* **H is the best answer because it has 7 weeks to work with, and you can shorten it by 5 weeks without altering the critical path** *(and affecting more work). we'd probably crash "I" by 2 weeks before we moved to B and L.*

10. Assuming the crash table information in the table that follows to be correct, what are the best crash priorities based purely on cost? *I followed by B and L.*

## Crash Table

The priority items for crashing are as shown below:

| Task | Current Duration | Cost | Compressed Duration | Cost | Weekly cost to compress (crash cost) | |
|------|------------------|------|---------------------|------|--------------------------------------|----|
| A | 7 | $1,000 | 3 | $5,000 | | |
| B | 8 | $22,000 | 4 | $30,000 | $2,000 | #3 |
| C | 6 | $3,000 | 5 | $4,000 | | |
| D | 6 | $5,000 | 6 | $5,000 | | |
| E | 6 | $11,000 | 4 | $17,000 | $3,000 | #4 |
| F | 8 | $1,000 | 7 | $2,000 | | |
| G | 4 | $5,000 | 2 | $8,000 | | |
| H | 7 | $10,000 | 3 | $25,000 | $3,750 | #5 |
| I | 3 | $1,000 | 2 | $2,000 | $1,000 | #1 |
| J | 3 | $5,000 | 2 | $6,000 | | |
| K | 2 | $1,000 | 1 | $1,500 | | |
| L | 5 | $10,000 | 2 | $16,000 | $2,000 | #2 |

## 21. Quality Plan

### Quality Terminology Crossword Puzzle

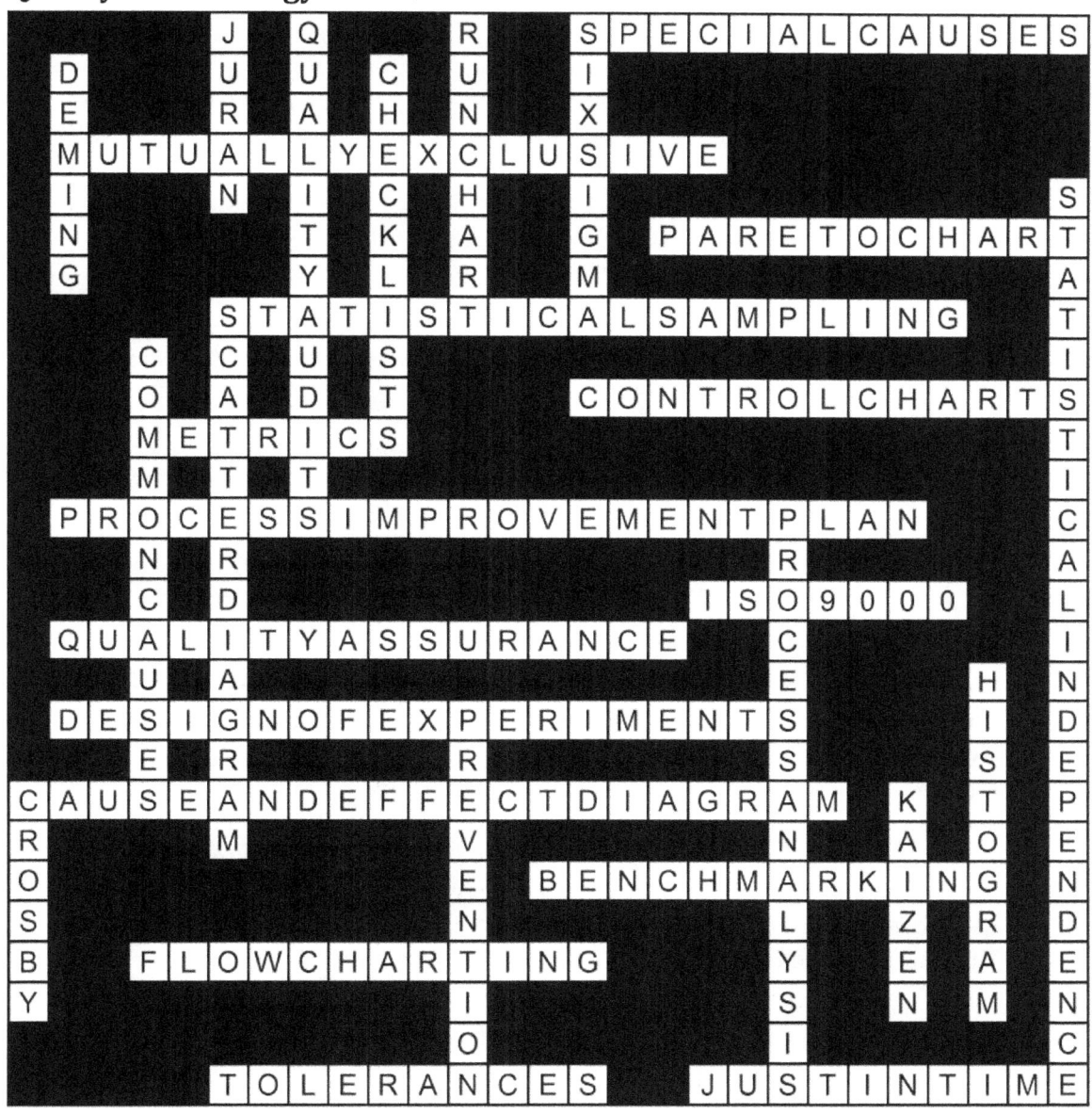

## 38. Schedule Control

Look at this schedule as compared to its baseline. If today is August 6th, what observations do you have related to schedule status from this chart?

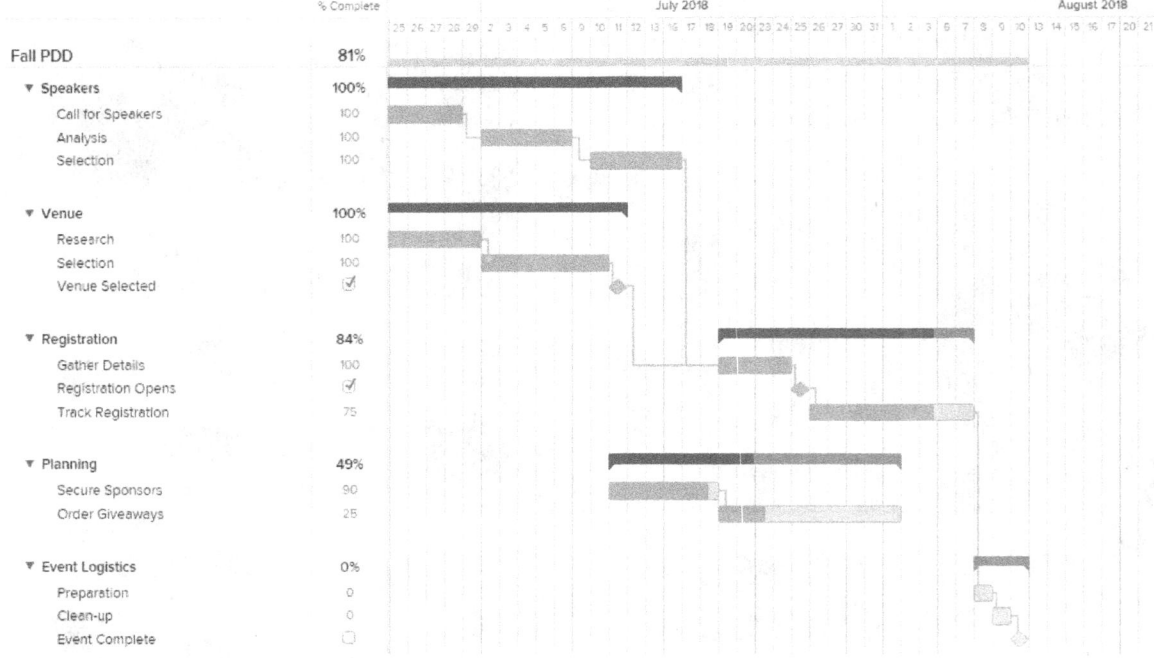

- We are on track for speakers and venue items.
- We still have not completed all tasks related to securing sponsors and ordering giveaways.
- If our event is on August 8th and today the August 6th, we are in jeopardy of not having sponsors secured and the giveaways in place for the event. This would be a critical risk.
- It appears that we still have time to resolve the final item related to secure sponsors if we take proactive measures. But, for the order giveaways, we are a week behind. We need to implement risk response strategies we had in place for the giveaway activity. This may have been to find the items locally and/or to forego any specialty printing.

# 42. Quality Control
**Practice This**

You are creating a new toy product. You use a check sheet to collect information related to quality. Two production runs have been completed with the results below.

| Defects/Date | Date Run 1 (9/1) | Date Run 2 (10/1) | Total |
| --- | --- | --- | --- |
| Small Scratches | 1 | 5 | 6 |
| Wrong Color | 2 | 3 | 5 |
| Missing Components | 0 | 0 | 0 |
| Labeling Error | 5 | 1 | 6 |

What observations concerning quality do you have related to this data?

- The incidences of scratches are increasing.
- Wrong color continues to be an issue.
- There have been no issues with missing components
- Labeling errors have decreased in the second run.

What might you try before the next run to improve quality?
- Examine the problem areas more closely to see if you can identify their cause.
- Talk with your SMEs to see if they have ideas that might improve quality.
- You may want to determine if additional training is needed.
- You may want to see if the machine(s) is calibrated correctly.

## 44. Cost Monitoring & Control

## Earned Value Drill

| BCWP (EV) | BCWS (PV) | ACWP (AC) | SITUATION ||||
|---|---|---|---|---|---|---|
| | | | AHEAD OF SCHEDULE | BEHIND SCHEDULE | COST UNDERRUN | COST OVERRUN |
| 7000 | 9000 | 7000 | | -2000 | 0 | 0 |
| 7000 | 6000 | 5000 | 1000 | | 2000 | |
| 3000 | 3000 | 6000 | 0 | 0 | | -3000 |
| 5000 | 7000 | 6000 | | -2000 | | -1000 |
| 7000 | 8000 | 7000 | | -1000 | 0 | 0 |
| 9000 | 6000 | 8000 | 3000 | | 1000 | |
| 4000 | 3000 | 5000 | 1000 | | | -1000 |
| 6000 | 7000 | 5000 | | -1000 | 1000 | |
| 2000 | 3000 | 4000 | | -1000 | | -2000 |
| 8000 | 6000 | 6000 | 2000 | | 2000 | |
| 7000 | 9000 | 9000 | | -2000 | | -2000 |
| 5000 | 5000 | 8000 | 0 | 0 | | -3000 |
| 5000 | 4000 | 3000 | 1000 | | 2000 | |
| 9000 | 7000 | 8000 | 2000 | | 1000 | |
| 5000 | 5000 | 5000 | 0 | 0 | 0 | 0 |
| 8000 | 9000 | 7000 | | -1000 | 1000 | |
| 5000 | 4000 | 6000 | 1000 | | | -1000 |
| 9000 | 7000 | 7000 | 2000 | | 2000 | |
| 1000 | 2000 | 2000 | | -1000 | | -1000 |

Watch this short video to help you with the fundamental concepts of Earned Value.
Video by Aileen Ellis - https://www.youtube.com/watch?v=U313VMm2r7Q

# Appendix A – Templates

Successful Projects has created the templates below to provide you with examples of some of the key documents you will want to use on your project. As a purchaser of this workbook, these templates are free for you to copy and use on your project and within your organization. We hope that you find this template set useful and welcome your comments. Public distribution of these documents is only permitted from the Successful Projects' official website at https://successfulprojects.com.

To access the templates, please visit:
https://successfulprojects.com/project-management-templates/
Password: sp!templates

1. Project Roadmap (for printing in color)
2. Project Charter
3. Project Scope Statement
4. WBS
5. Project Budget
6. RACI Chart
7. Risk Register
8. Risk Control Form
9. Change Request Form
10. Communication Plan
11. Deliverable Acceptance Form
12. WBS Dictionary
13. Status Report
14. Contract Performance Management Template
15. Issue Log
16. Lessons Learned Questions

# Appendix B – Recommended Reading List

- Brooks, F. P. (1995). *The Mythical Man Month: Essays on Software Engineering* (Anniversary Edition). Addison-Wesley Longman Inc.
- Martinelli, R.M. and Milosevic, D.Z. (2016). *Project Management Toolbox: Tools and Techniques for the Practicing Project Manager* (2$^{nd}$ Edition). Hoboken, NJ: John Wiley & Sons, Inc.
- Foster, S.T. (2003). *Managing Quality: An Integrative Approach* (2$^{nd}$ Edition). Prentice Hall
- Takeuchi, Hirotaka, and Ikujiro Nonaka. *The New New Product Development Game*. Harvard Business Review 64, no. 1 (January–February 1986).
- Kerzner, Harold. (2017). *Project Management: A Systems Approach to Planning, Scheduling, and Controlling* (12$^{th}$ Edition). Hoboken, NJ: John Wiley & Sons, Inc.
- Project Management Institute. (2006). *Practice Standard for Work Breakdown Structures*
- Project Management Institute. (2017). A Guide to the *Project Management Body of Knowledge*. (6$^{th}$ Edition)
- Kaner, Sam. (2014). *Facilitator's Guide to Participatory Decision-Making*, (3rd Edition). ISBN 978-1-118-40495-9. Jossey-Bass
- Weiss, Tara. (2007). *How to Hold a Great Meetings*. Forbes Article
- Bilanich, Bud. (2005). *Solving Performance Problems…A Leaders Toolkit*. Walk the Talk
- Verzuth, Eric. (2015) *Fast Forward MBA in Project Management* (5$^{th}$ Edition). Hoboken, NJ: John Wiley & Sons, Inc.
- Bradberry, Travis and Greaves, Jean. (2009). *Emotional Intelligence 2.0*. Talent Smart.
- Adair, Renee. (2018). *Success-PM: PMP Exam Study Guide and Workbook*.